Mike k
Aug. 1

MW00772087

Cosmic and Human Metamorphoses

Rudolf Steiner, 1916

COSMIC & HUMAN METAMORPHOSES

7 lectures in Berlin, February 6, 1917 to March 20, 1917

RUDOLF STEINER

SteinerBooks | 2012

2012
SteinerBooks

An imprint of Anthroposophic Press, Inc.
610 Main St., Great Barrington, MA 01230
www.steinerbooks.org

Translated from the German-language book *Bausteine zu Einer Erkenntnis des Mysteriums von Golgatha. Kosmische und menschliche Metamorphose* (17 lectures in Berlin) in the Collected Edition of Rudolf Steiner's Works, no. 175, Bibliographical Survey, 1961, Rudolf Steiner Nachlassverwaltung, Dornach, Switzerland.

Copyright © 2012 by SteinerBooks (Anthroposophic Press, Inc.) All rights reserved. No part of this book may be reproduced in any form without the written permission of the publishers, except for brief quotations embodied in critical articles and reviews.

Cover and book design; William ,Jens ,Jensen

LIBRARY OF CONGRESS CATALOGING-IN-PUBLICATION DATA

Steiner, Rudolf, 1861–1925.

[Bausteine zu einer Erkenntnis des Mysteriums von Golgatha. English]

Cosmic and human metamorphoses : 7 lectures in Berlin, February 6, 1917 to March 20, 1917 / Rudolf Steiner.

p. cm.

Includes bibliographical references.

ISBN 978-1-62148-000-6

eBook ISBN: 978-1-62148-001-3

1. Anthroposophy. I. Title.

BP595.S894B3813 2012

299'.935—dc23

2012002761

CONTENTS

MATERIALISM AND SPIRITUALITY— LIFE AND DEATH

Berlin, February 6, 1917

Let us turn our thoughts, dear friends, as we continually do, to the guardian spirits of those who are absent from us, taking their place where the great destinies of the time are being fulfilled:

> Spirits ever watchful, Guardian of their souls!
> May your vibrations waft
> To the Earth human beings committed to your charge
> Our souls' petitioning love:
> That, united with your power,
> Our prayer may helpfully radiate
> To the souls it lovingly seeks!

And to the spirits of those who have passed through the gate of death:

> Spirits ever watchful, Guardians of their souls!
> May your vibrations waft
> To human beings of the spheres committed to your
>   charge
> Our souls' petitioning love:
> That, united with your power,
> Our prayer may helpfully radiate
> To the souls it lovingly seeks!

And that Spirit, Who for the healing of the Earth
    and for her progress, and for the freedom
    and salvation of humankind, passed through
    the Mystery of Golgotha;
The Spirit whom in our spiritual science we seek,
    to whom we would draw near,
May he be at your side in all your difficult tasks![1]

Let me first express the deep satisfaction I have in being able to be once more in your midst. I would have come earlier, but for an urgent need, that kept me in Dornach until the work on "The Group" had reached a point at which it could be continued without me. You have often heard me speak of "The Group," which will stand in the east end of the Goetheanum and presents the Representative of Humanity in relation to ahrimanic forces on the one hand, and on the other to luciferic forces. These days, one needs forethought for the future, and it seemed to me absolutely necessary, considering what may happen, to make that progress with "The Group" before leaving Dornach, which has now been possible. Furthermore, the times are certain to bring home to us with particular intensity the fact that meeting with one another here on the physical plane is not the only thing that sustains and strengthens us in the impulse of spiritual science. Rather, we must be born up through this difficult time of sorrow and trial by coming together in our anthroposophic efforts, even if together only in spirit. And indeed, this very thing is to be the test for our anthroposophic efforts.

Since we were together here previously, we have had to lament the loss from the physical plane of our dear Ms. Motzkus, as well as other dear friends who have left the physical plane because of the current terrible events. It is especially painful to see Ms. Motzkus no longer among the friends who have shared our anthroposophic efforts here for so many years. She had been

---

1   These meditations were repeated at the beginning of each lecture in the series.

a member of our movement since its beginning. From the first day, from the first meeting of a very small circle, she always showed the deepest and most heartfelt devotion to our movement and participated intimately and earnestly in all the phases it went through, in all its times of trial and testing. Above all, through the events and changes through which we had to pass, she preserved an invincible loyalty to the movement in the deepest sense of the word—loyalty through which she set an example to all those who would wish to be worthy members of the anthroposophic movement. Thus, with our gaze we follow this beloved and pure soul into the spiritual worlds to which she has ascended, still feeling toward her the bond of trust and confidence that has grown stronger and deeper over the years, knowing that our own souls are linked with hers forever....

Recently, Ms. Motzkus herself suffered the loss of a dear friend, whom she quickly found again in the spiritual world. She bore that sad blow in such a way that it could be received and born by one who is conscious of an actual hold on the spiritual world. It was marvelous to witness Ms. Motzkus's ardent and intense interest in the great events of our time, right up to the last days of her life. She told me repeatedly that she would like to remain here on the physical plane until the momentous events, in the midst of which we are living, have reached a decisive conclusion. Now she will be able to follow these events to which she has been so closely and intimately linked with even freer vision and firmer impulse for the evolution of humanity. May it be laid on all our hearts to unite ourselves whenever we can in thought and in soul activity with this faithful spirit, a faithful and well-loved member of our movement. In this way, we who have been so remarkably united with her here on the physical plane will continue to know that we are united with her in the years to come, when she will be among us in another form.

The times in which we live are such that it is becoming increasingly an urgent matter to understand the struggle for spiritual knowledge and its significance for the humanity today and in the immediate future. The events in the midst of which we now stand cause a sort of numbing in many today, though it is little noticed. The souls who survive the catastrophe on the physical plane will not awake until later to recognize fully what is happening and realize how deeply this catastrophe has cut into human evolution. Moreover, we should feel the need to evoke illuminating thoughts in our souls that can shed light on the objects and aims of the spiritual movement so needed by humanity. In addition, since we have come together now after so long, it may be useful to specify the views of our spiritual science in a few short thoughts—or rather the views that naturally arise as a result of the spiritual science we have had before our souls for some years. It is clear that in all parts of the world there are some members of humanity who are developing a longing to approach the spiritual world, despite the fact that materialism is unfortunately not decreasing, and because of the various forms that such longing for the spirit is taking. Consequently, we must specify and bring our own search for spiritual life before the soul. In England today, research into the spiritual world by one of the most prominent and learned individuals is making a great impression in large circles, even those of cultured people.

It is an extraordinary phenomenon that a man considered to be among the first scientists of that country should have written a comprehensive book about the relationship between human beings on Earth and the spiritual world, and that this should have taken such a remarkable form. In this book, Sir Oliver Lodge[2] (who for some years has worked in various ways to extend the scientific knowledge he acquired so that it may be applied to the spiritual world) describes a series of episodes in which he asserts that he has come in touch with the spiritual world. The case is as follows. Sir Oliver Lodge had a son, Raymond, who in 1915 took part on the English side during the war in Flanders. At a

---

2 Sir Oliver Joseph Lodge (1851–1940) was a physicist and writer who helped develop key patents in wireless telegraphy.

time when his parents knew him to be at the front, they received remarkable news from America, which to those having what I might call "materialistic spiritualistic" tendencies must certainly have seemed very striking. The message supposedly came from the English psychologist Frederick Myers (1843–1901), who before his death many years ago had studied the relationship between the physical and spiritual worlds, and who himself, now in the spiritual world, pronounced that world would soon be prepared to receive young Lodge. At first, it was not clear to what the message referred. There was some delay before the message reached Sir Oliver—only after his son had fallen. I think it was two weeks later, but I am not certain.

Then other messages came, given through mediums in America, advising the parents to go to an English medium. Consequently, Sir Oliver did visit one, though he maintained a skeptical attitude toward her. (I will have more to say on the significance of this.) Sir Oliver is a scientist, trained for the scientific testing of such cases. He went to work as he would in his laboratory, and what follows was given not through one but several mediums. The soul of Raymond wanted to communicate with the Lodge family. All sorts of communications followed through automatic writing and table turning communications. It was so surprising that not only Sir Oliver himself, but also the rest of the family became quite convinced, though they had been extremely skeptical in such matters.

Among other statements, the soul of Raymond stated that Myers was with him and acting as a guardian. He told them several things about his final days on Earth, and much that was significant to the parents and family, making a great impression upon them, especially as various things communicated by Raymond through mediums were intended for the family, particularly for Sir Oliver. The way the sittings were held afforded great surprise to the family, and strangely enough, they also caused great surprise to a wide public. They would not have surprised anyone who had experience of such things, since, in reality, the nature of the communications concerning the dead that comes through mediums and the manner of the communication is quite familiar to the investigator.

One thing, however, made a profound impression in England, and was well calculated to impress and convince the civilized world of England and America and to bring conviction thus far lacking to many in our skeptical age. This fact, which converted many and will convert many more, made a very strong impression on the Lodge family, particularly Sir Oliver, and impressed much of the public. It was the following incident.

A description was given through a medium of some photographs taken while Raymond was still alive. Raymond himself described them to the medium by means of rapping.[3] In this way, a photographic group was described—that is, by means of the medium the soul of Raymond was evidently trying to describe the photograph taken of him in a group shortly before he passed through the gates of death. From the other side, he told them that he had sat in two groups with his companions and that these were taken one after the other, describing his position in the groups. Furthermore, he described the differences in the two different photographs, saying that he sat on the same chair and in the same attitude in both, but that the position of the arm was a little different and so on.

All this was described in detail. Now the family knew nothing of these photographs; they did not know that any such had been taken. Thus, indirectly through the medium, the fact was made known that there was a photographic group in existence representing Raymond Lodge with several companions. Some few weeks later, a photograph was sent to Sir Oliver from France, corresponding exactly to the one described by the soul of Raymond through the medium. This would naturally make

---

3   The Spiritualism movement began with what was termed *typtology*, a mode of spirit communication in which spirits lift and tilt a table during a séance to produce rapping sounds. See, for example, Rudolf Steiner, *Spiritualism, Madame Blavatsky and Theosophy*.

a strong impression on anyone who approaches such things in a superficial way, as all those concerned clearly did. It was an experimental test.

The case in point is that of a soul from the other side who described photographs, several copies of which reached the family some time later. They were then found to correspond in every detail to the description given. It was quite impossible that either the medium or anyone present at the sittings could have seen the photographs. We have a case that must be addressed both scientifically and historically; not only might we say that such a case would naturally make a great impression, but also that it really did occur and made an enormous impression. As far as could be seen, this photographic proof, which has nothing to do with thought transference, was very convincing.

It is necessary for us to bring the whole of this case before our mind's vision. We must be quite clear about the fact that, when a human being passes through the gate of death, the human individuality is at first briefly enshrouded in the astral and ether bodies; and that the latter after a more or less brief period—varying in different cases, but never lasting more than a few days—passes out into the etheric world and there pursues its further destiny; so that the individuality enters the spiritual world with the astral body only, and continues its further wanderings in that world. The ether body is severed from the human individuality just as the physical body was on Earth.

Now we must clearly understand that in spiritualistic séances (and the whole work of Sir Oliver Lodge is based on these), only a person who has real knowledge can determine whether the communications come from the actual individuality or merely from the castoff, forsaken etheric corpse. This etheric corpse remains in continual communication with the individuality. However, when one makes a connection with the spiritual world in a roundabout way through a medium, one comes in touch with the etheric corpse first, and so can never be sure of reaching the actual individual in this way. It is certain in our age that there is an effort to find some sort of proof for spiritual existence, such as is found by experiments in the laboratory, something that can be grasped with hands and that one can actually see in the material world. Our materialistic age does not care about following the inner path that the soul must take in the spiritual worlds, the purely spiritual path; it wants the spirit to descend into the material world and be discovered there. We are experiencing all kinds of materialistic spiritualism, a materialistic turning to the worlds of the spirit.

Now, it is quite possible for the ether body, which has been separated from the actual human individuality, to manifest a certain life of its own which, to the uninitiated, may easily be mistaken for the life of the individual himself. We must not think that the ether body when given over to the etheric world only manifests reminiscences and recollections, mere echoes of what the human being passes through here; it manifests a real continuous individuality. It can relate incidents and say quite new things, but we should be going quite off the track if we thought that because a connection is established with the ether body, we are necessarily in connection with the individual himself. It is very possible in the case of people sitting in a small circle—all being members of the family as was the case with the Lodges, all thinking in one way or another about the dead human being, and all filled with thoughts and memories of him—that their thoughts may be conveyed to his ether body through the medium, and that this ether body may occasionally give striking replies, which may actually produce the impression of being spoken by the individuality of the dead. Yet, perhaps, they may only proceed from his etheric corpse. Those who are acquainted with such things actually find this to be the case, and when Raymond Lodge was supposed to come to his family through the medium, in reality it was the etheric corpse speaking. Raymond Lodge had not really held communion with the circle at all. Hence, as I have said, to those accustomed to the course of events in such séances, the communications do not appear very remarkable.

It is likely that the whole story would not have made such an impression on a wider public, nor would it continue to do so, had it not been for the incident of the photographs. This story of the photographs is remarkable, indeed exceptionally so, because here it was impossible that any transference of thoughts should take place—passing through the medium to the ether body of Raymond, as might have been the case in the other instances. No one in England could have known of the photographs; they had not yet come over at the time of the communications. Nonetheless, it is still very strange that such a learned scientist as Sir Oliver Lodge, who had for so long been interesting himself in these matters, should not know how such a circumstance is to be regarded.

I have taken particular trouble to look into this case more minutely. Sir Oliver Lodge is an educated man and a scientist, upon whose descriptions one can rely. We are not dealing with any ordinary document produced by ordinary spiritualistic séances, but with the communications of a person describing with the certainty of a scientist, who has developed the conscientiousness customary to a scientist in the laboratory; therefore, it is possible to form a complete picture of what happened from his descriptions. It is remarkable that a learned man such as Sir Oliver Lodge was interested in the subject for so many years (although in this case he was specially interested because it was a question of his own son), yet would not have known what has often been mentioned in our spiritual science when describing atavistic forms of clairvoyance that manifest as presentiments. For this is none other than a very special case of deuteroscopy,[4] as follows.

We have a medium, and the spiritual world is in a certain sense accessible to this medium. Of course, as we know (through atavistic forces), such mediums can reach beyond space in their vision, but not only does their so-called second sight extend beyond space,

---

4   *Deuteroscopy* = second sight, or spiritual vision.

it also extends beyond time. Let us consider a special case—one quoted hundreds of times. You may read descriptions of it if you have not experienced it yourself through your acquaintances.

The case I refer to is when someone who has that tendency sees one's coffin or funeral, as in a dream or half in a vision. Then this individual dies two weeks later. One saw in advance what was to occur fourteen days later. Or, perhaps, one may see not one's own funeral or coffin, but that of a complete stranger, an event in which the dreamer has no interest. In a particular case, one may see oneself leaving the house and falling off a horse. This thing did occur—someone saw that happen and tried to avert it—but, notwithstanding all precautions, it nonetheless happened. That is a case of a vision extending in time, and what Sir Oliver Lodge describes is precisely this second sight in time. His descriptions are given so accurately that it was possible to investigate the case. Through her forces, the medium was able to see an event still in the future. At the time she spoke, the photograph was not present but arrived about two weeks later. It was then shown around to friends and relatives. This happened some time later, but the medium saw it in advance; it was a prophetic vision, a case of deuteroscopy. It was a prevision; that is the explanation. It had nothing to do with a communication between those on the physical plane and someone in the spiritual world.

You see how greatly one may be misled by striving to give a materialistic explanation of spiritual circumstances in the world, and how blind one may be to the actual facts; of course, such a vision is nonetheless a proof of the reality of a world behind the ordinary world of sense. The case is an interesting one; only it should not be quoted as proving a connection between the dead and the living. We must seek for the dead—if indeed we should or ought to seek for them at all—by following a truly spiritual path. In the near future I shall have many things to say on this subject; for it is my intention to give much consideration to the subject of the relation between the living and the dead.

I have brought up the subject of this book of Sir Oliver Lodge to show you how, although the longing after the spiritual world does exist, it may here be said to have taken a materialistic form. Sir Oliver Lodge is a learned scientist; although he strives after the spiritual world, he tries to gain knowledge of it by methods of the chemical world or of physics. Just as he experiments in his laboratory according to the laws of chemistry, so he wants visual proof of what relates to the spiritual world. But the way we must recognize as the right one is very far from his; our way leads the soul by an inner method to the spiritual world, as we have often described, and no less often have we described what the soul first becomes acquainted with there and which immediately concerns us at the present time and underlies the world of physical sense, in which we live. We learn to recognize the whole materialistic character of our age, in the materialistic efforts that are directed to the spiritual world. If our movement is to have any meaning at all, a meaning which it should eventually have in accordance with the necessary evolutionary laws of humankind, it must sharply define and emphasize the spiritual inwardness of true spirituality, as compared with these materialistic and absurd efforts after a world of spirit.

Now, such an event as this cannot come quite suddenly, even as the event of Golgotha did not come suddenly but was prepared for during thirty-three years. The point of time when the event is to occur—this time spiritually—is very near and will have a like significance for humanity as the event of Golgotha on the physical plane. Hence, if you consider the facts alluded to above, you will not find it difficult to believe me when I say *said in 1917* that He is already present in the form in which He will be seen in the great moment of evolution in the twentieth century, that the great moment is being now prepared. You will not consider it incredible, when I say that moment is now being prepared. Yes, we may say that although humanity seems as regards its present actions far from being permeated with the Christ spirit on the physical plane, yet if human souls will but open themselves

11

to him, the Christ, who is now approaching, is very near. The occultist is able to point out that since the year 1909 or there-abouts what is to come is being distinctly and perceptibly pre-pared for, that since the year 1909 we are inwardly living in a very special time. It is possible today, if we do but seek him, to be very near to Christ, to find Him in a quite different way than has been hitherto possible.

Why is it necessary in the present age that an entirely new method should hold human hearts, a purely spiritual method, one very different from the materialistic methods? This ques-tion must be considered in connection with the fact to which we have often alluded in the course of past years, and which must closely concern us at this time of sorrow and trial. We have indicated that this twentieth century must bring to humanity the vision of the etheric Christ. It truly happened (as we have often said) that at the time of the Mystery of Golgotha, Christ walked among humanity in a physical form in one known part of the Earth. Likewise, the etheric Christ will walk among human beings over the whole Earth during the twentieth cen-tury. This event must not pass unobserved by humanity, for that would be sinning against the salvation of the world. Humanity must have its attention roused, so that a sufficient number of persons may actually be ready to see the Christ who will come and who must be seen.

There is one thought that occurs to me, and simple as it may seem I must give words to it, from a profound feeling for the times. People do not, alas, as a rule, think with sufficient clear-ness on the events of the past; especially with respect to what took place in human souls in bygone centuries; they no longer have any concept of the strength of the impression made by the Gospels in their existing form upon a circle that was then quite small. People now have no concept of how powerfully these ideas filled human souls at that time. As the centuries rolled by, the impression made by the inner substance of the Gospels grew con-tinually weaker. Today, if we see things as they are, we can say that, although individuals who possess certain powers of intuition and forces of divination may be permeated by the words of the Gospels enough to form some idea of what took place at the time of the Mystery of Golgotha, the immense force once possessed by the Gospel words themselves is nevertheless growing weaker and weaker, and we have to see that the Gospels now make only a minor impression on most people.

This is not readily accepted, but it is the truth, so it would be better if people could realize it. How did this condition come about? Just as it is true that what pulsed in the Gospels is not an earthly language but cosmic words, heavenly words, possessing an immeasurably greater force than anything else on Earth, likewise it is also true that humankind in our time has become estranged from the form of these words as laid down in the Gospels at the time of the Mystery of Golgotha. Just consider how enormously difficult it is to understand when you encounter the language of even four or five hundred years ago. It is impossible to draw out its true content. The Gospels, as we find them today, are not actually the original Gospels; they do not possess their original force. It is possible to penetrate them, as I have said, by means of a kind of intuition, but they no longer have the same force. Christ spoke the word that should be deeply engraved in the human soul: "I am with you always, even unto the end of the Earth time" (Matt. 28:20). That is a truth, a fact. He will be with us in various forms close to the human soul during the time indicated in the twentieth century.

From what I have said, you will understand that those who feel they are standing in the center of these matters, those who are esotericists, should say that Christ is here; he makes his presence felt in such a way that we know clearly that he will now expect more of his human children than in bygone centuries. Until now, the Gospels have spoken an inner language to human beings. They had to take hold of the soul; people should therefore be satisfied with faith alone and need not progress to knowledge. That time is now over; it lies behind us. Christ has something different in view for his human children. His present purpose is that the kingdom to which he referred when he said "My kingdom is not of this world" (John 18:36) should really draw the part of the human being that is not of this world but of another. In each of us, there is a part that is not of this world. The part of human beings that is not of this world must seek with intensity the kingdom of which Christ spoke and described it as not of this world.

We are living at a time when this must be understood. Many such things in human evolution announce themselves through contrasts. In our own age something great and significant is announced by a great contrast. With the coming Christ, with the presence of Christ, will come the time when people will learn to inquire of him, not only concerning their souls, but concerning their immortal part on Earth. Christ is not merely a ruler of humankind, but also our brother, who, particularly in the near future, wishes to be consulted on all the details of life. In anything we undertake today, we act in the opposite way. Events seem to be accomplished today, in which people seem to be removed as far as possible from any appeal to Christ.

We must ask, who stops today to ask: What would Jesus Christ say about what is taking place now? Who asks themselves such a question? Many say they do, but it would be sacrilegious to believe that they put the question in this form, addressing it directly to Christ himself. Yet, the time must come and cannot be far when human souls will, in their immortal part, inquire of Christ when they think of some undertaking: "Should we do this or not?" Then human souls will see Christ standing by them as the beloved companion, and they will not only obtain consolation and strength from the Christ being, but will also receive instruction from him about what to do.

The kingdom of Jesus Christ is not of this world, but it must work in this world and human souls must be instruments of the Kingdom that is not of this world. From this point of view, we must consider the fact of how few today have asked themselves the question that, regarding individual acts and events, must be put to the Christ. Humanity must, however, learn to ask of him.

How is that to come about? It can become possible only if we learn his language. Those who comprehend the deeper purpose of our spiritual science realize that it not only gives theoretical knowledge about the various problems of humanity, the principles of human nature, reincarnation and karma, but also that it contains a quite special language, that it has a particular way of expressing itself about spiritual matters. The fact that through spiritual science we learn to inwardly converse with the spiritual world in thought is much more important than the merely acquiring theoretical thoughts. Christ is with us always, even to the end of the earthly epochs, and we must learn his language. Through the language (no matter how abstract it seems) in which we hear of Saturn, Sun, Moon, and Earth and the various periods and ages of the Earth, as well as the many other secrets of evolution, we teach ourselves a language by which we can frame the questions we ask of the spiritual world. When we really learn inwardly to speak the language of this spiritual life, the result is that Christ will stand by us and give us the answers himself.

This is the attitude that our work in spiritual science should bring about in us, as a sentiment, a feeling. Why do we occupy ourselves with spiritual science? It is as though we were learning the vocabulary of the language through which we approach the Christ. If we take the trouble to learn how to think the thoughts of spiritual science and make the mental effort needed to understand the cosmic secrets taught by spiritual science, then, out of the dim, dark foundations of the cosmic mysteries, will arise the figure of Jesus Christ, which will draw near to us and give us the strength and force in which we shall then live. The Christ will guide us, standing beside us as a brother, so that our hearts and souls may be strong enough to grow up to the necessary level of the tasks awaiting humanity in its further development.

Let us then try to acquire spiritual science, not as a mere doctrine but as a language, and then wait until we can find in that language the questions we may venture to put to the Christ. He will answer—yes, indeed, he will answer! Plentiful indeed will be the soul forces, the soul-strengthening, the soul impulses that students will carry away with them from the gray spiritual depths through which humanity in its evolution is now passing, if they are able to receive instructions from Christ himself. In the near future, he will give instructions to those who seek.

METAMORPHOSES OF THE SOUL FORCES

Berlin, February 13, 1917

The lecture given here a week ago culminated with a fact
well-known to the spiritual investigator: Although the very
height of materialistic views and opinions prevail in the outer
world, we are nevertheless now entering an epoch of the dema-
terializing of thought and the world of ideas that must, in time,
lead to spiritualization and the permeation of earthly life as
such by the spirit. What must grasp and affect outer life on the
physical plane must be comprehended and understood spiritually—first by a few and then by an ever-increasing number of
people. In this sense, spiritual science should be a beginning
through which people can lift their souls to what is available
to those today who wish to rise to it, which is not yet reflected
by external physical life, though this is what must happen if
the Earth is to avoid, in a sense, being overtaken by the fall of
materialistic development.

The situation of human beings today can be described as
follows: The human soul, generally speaking, is actually very
close to the spiritual world. However, the ideas and especially
the feelings produced by a materialistic concept of the world
and by a materialistic attitude toward it have woven a veil to
cover what is in fact very close to the human soul today. The
connection between physical Earth existence, in which human
beings with their whole being are involved, notwithstanding

many assertions to the contrary made in other quarters—the connection between this materialistic Earth existence and the spiritual world can be found by human beings, if they try to develop the inner courageous forces needed for understanding, not only what nature paints to the outer senses, but also that which remains invisible. We can unite ourselves with this invisible essence and experience it, if we stir up the inner force of the soul sufficiently to become aware that in this force the soul shares in something superhuman and spiritual. This connection must not be sought just as human connections and relationships are sought, in the rude external sense existence; for the connection between the human soul and the spiritual world is to be found in the intimate forces which the human soul develops when it evolves an inner, silent and quiet attention. Human beings must now train themselves to this, for in this materialistic age we have become accustomed to paying attention only to what presses on us from without, and that in a sense calls out to our capacities of perception. The spirit that must be experienced within does not call out; we must wait for it, and we can approach it only by preparing ourselves for its approach.

Concerning matters of the external world that present themselves to our senses and press in on our outer perception, we can say that they come to us, they speak to us, but we cannot say anything of the kind about the way the spirit, the spiritual world, approaches us. The language of modern times (as I have often said) is more or less coined for the use of the external world, and it is therefore difficult to find words to convey a real impression of the part of the spiritual world that stands before the soul. However, we can attempt to show the approximate difference between that and the physical. We might say that the spiritual is experienced in the feeling of gratitude that comes whenever we experience the spiritual—we feel grateful to it.

Make a special note of this; *we owe gratitude to the spiritual world*. By observing the physical world, we say that we see the mineral world spread before our senses, from which arise the

18

worlds of plant, animal, and us—the world of human beings. In the latter we feel in a sense that we are at the top of an ascending sequence of outer kingdoms, whereas in terms of the spiritual kingdoms, we feel we are at the bottom. Above and beyond us stretch the kingdoms of the angels, archangels, archai, and so on. We feel the whole time that we are being supported from these kingdoms, continually called to life by them. We owe gratitude to them. We look up to them and say that our lives and the whole content of our souls flow down to us from the will-impregnated thoughts of the beings belonging to those worlds, and by them we are constantly being formed. This feeling of personal gratitude to the higher kingdoms should become just as alive in us as, say, feeling the impressions received through physical perception. When these two feelings are equally alive in our souls—one in which external sensory phenomena react upon us, and the other to which we owe what lives in the very center of our being to the higher hierarchies—the soul is then in a state of balance in which it can continually and correctly perceive the cooperative activity of the spiritual and the physical, which continues unceasingly but cannot be perceived unless the two feelings described here are properly balanced.

There are also other moments in life when, I might say, it is possible for the spiritual world to penetrate to us. Each time we develop a thought so that it springs from ourselves, when we take the initiative, when we are confronted with a decision to be made by ourselves, even in small things, that again is a favorable moment for the approach of the dead karmically connected with us. Of course if we simply surrender ourselves up, allowing life to take its course and carry us along with the stream, there is little likelihood of the true, inwardly living spiritual world working into us. Such moments are not necessarily "important" in the sense we attach to the word in ordinary material life; very often, what is really important as a spiritual experience would seem unimportant for the outer life; but to those who are able to see into these things, it is extremely clear that such experiences, perhaps outwardly unimportant yet exceptionally important inwardly, are profoundly related to our karma.

Thus, it is necessary to notice even very intimate soul occurrences if one desires to attain an understanding of the spiritual world. For instance, it may happen that a human being sitting in one's room or walking in the street may be startled by an unexpected sound, perhaps a crack or a bang. After a fright, one may have a moment of musing, during which something important is revealed from the spiritual world. It is necessary to pay attention to these things; as a rule, one is concerned only with the fright; one continues to think only of the shock. That is why it is so important to acquire "inner balance" as indicated at the end of the book *Theosophy* and in *How to Know Higher Worlds*.[1] Once that has been acquired, we are no longer so perplexed after a shock that we think of nothing else; we will have mastery over ourselves and may be able to call up, though perhaps only faintly, what we experienced in such seemingly unimportant but in fact extremely important moments. Such things are of course mere beginnings and must develop further. When we develop the two capacities—that of *attentiveness at the moment of awaking* and that of *attentiveness at the moment when we are shaken by some outer occurrence*, we will again be able to find the connection with the great cosmos, which is composed of both substance and spirit, of which we are members and from which we arose—indeed, arose to become free human beings, but from which we most certainly emerged. In reality, the belief of primeval human beings was correct; we do not wander about the Earth like hermits, as is now believed. What primeval human beings believed is true—that humankind is a member of the whole great cosmic connection, as each one of our fingers is a member of our whole organism. People no longer possess this feeling today—at least the great majority no longer feel they are members of the great world organism,

---

1   See, for example, *How to Know Higher Worlds*, chapter 5, "Requirements for Esoteric Training," pp. 95–107.

insofar as they are spiritual beings living in a visible world. Yet ordinary scientific reflection might teach a human being, even today, that he and his life are part of the whole cosmic ordering in which he as organism is placed.

Let us take a simple example that needs only very simple reasoning. We all know that in the spring, on March 21, the Sun rises at a definite point in the heavens. We call this the "vernal point." We know, too, that this vernal point is not the same each year, but that it progresses. We know that now the Sun rises in Pisces. Until the fifteenth century, it rose in Aries (astronomy continues to say "in Aries," which is incorrect, but this remark does not apply at the moment.) Thus the vernal point progresses; the Sun rises a little further on in the zodiac each spring, and it is easy to see that eventually it will have moved through the whole zodiac. The place of sunrise will have moved through the whole zodiac. Now the approximate time needed for the Sun in its journey through the zodiac is 25,920 years. Therefore, taking the vernal point of any given year, it will be further along the year following, and the year after will have progressed again. When 25,920 years have passed, the vernal point will be back at its original position. Thus, 25,920 years is an exceptionally important space of time in our Solar System; the Sun has accomplished what I might call a cosmic step, when at the vernal ascent it returns to the same point. Now Plato, the great Greek philosopher, called these 25,920 years a cosmic year, the great Platonic cosmic year. If one has not gone deeply into all this, what I am about to say will only seem astonishing; it is indeed astonishing, but at the same time filled with profound significance.

From now on into the future, evolution must proceed in such a way that, through the presence of these two feelings in the human soul, additional forces will be "super-added," forces that are unable to grow there in the present materialistic age. It is of course understood that what is meant here refers to something that has greatly altered over the course of human development. Only at the early primeval stages of human development was there a connection with the spiritual world, and indeed that was only dim and unconscious. At the primeval time of human development, human beings had not just the two states we now have, those of sleeping and waking and, between these, a chaotic dreamy state. There was then a third state in which reality was present. This was not merely a state of dreaming, for in it humankind was able (though human consciousness was dampened down) to see pictures and to learn through them, for those pictures were true to spiritual reality. As we know, in order for human beings to develop the full earthly consciousness, this means of perception had to be withdrawn. Had it persisted, human beings would never have gained their freedom; we could not have become free if we had not been subjected to all the dangers, arguments, and temptations of materialism. Nevertheless, human beings must find their way back again to the spiritual world and must now be able to grasp it in full earthly consciousness. This is connected with far-reaching and complicated concepts that have altered with everything else that has changed in human evolution, as indicated.

In primal ages, it was quite natural to live in constant communion with souls departed from this physical life. Proof of this was unnecessary then; in the state of consciousness in which human beings perceived the spiritual world through pictures, they lived in the company of those with whom they were in some way connected by karma and who had passed into the spiritual world through the portal of death. The existence of the dead was personal knowledge to them; people knew they were not dead but alive and living in a different form of existence. Something needs no proof if one knows it!

In those early times there was no need to discuss immortality or to wonder about it; human beings had personal experience of the so-called dead. Moreover, communion with the dead had other and far-reaching results. It was then easier to the dead themselves to work through human beings. I do not say this cannot be done now; it can still be done in this way, but I do say it was easier then for the dead to find ways of working through humankind here on Earth, and thus to participate in events here. In those primeval ages, the dead were active in the impulses of people's will; in all that people understood and did, the dead participated, thus helping to bring about what took place on Earth. Materialism has not only brought materialistic ideas, which would be its least harmful accomplishment, it has also brought about a completely different form of union with the spiritual world. It is now possible only to a much more restricted degree for the so-called dead to take part in earthly evolution through the so-called living.

However, humankind will have to return to their connection with the dead, but this will be possible only when to some extent people come to understand the language of the dead, and this language is none other than that of spiritual science. It may certainly appear, at first sight, as though spiritual science tells us only more or less of spiritual erudition, of evolving worlds, of human evolution, of the various principles composing human nature—matters in which perhaps some people are not interested, wishing rather for something calculated to set their hearts and feelings aglow. Certainly it is a good thing to want that, but the question is how far the satisfaction of that demand will take us.

It may seem as though spiritual science teaches us only how the Earth evolved and developed through ancient Saturn, Sun, and Moon, how the different epochs of civilization developed on Earth, and how the various principles of the human being were added. But while we devote ourselves to these seemingly abstract though in fact concrete thoughts, endeavoring to think in such a way that these things really remain in our minds as pictures, we are actually learning in a definite way to form certain thoughts and ideas that we could not have brought into our souls in any other way. If we have the right feelings and realize how our ideas have changed since we busied ourselves with the subject of spiritual science, the time will come when we will consider it just as absurd to say that these things do not interest us as it would be for children to say they have no interest in learning the A-B-Cs, wishing instead to learn only to speak.

What children must experience in their physical existence while learning to speak is abstract compared to what the living language can communicate, just as the ideas pertaining to spiritual science are abstract compared to the thoughts, ideas, and feelings aroused in the soul under the influence of these concepts. Of course this requires patience, and it is necessary that we consider not what spiritual science has to offer merely in the abstract, but take the whole life into account. That, however, in terms of what we are now considering, does not suggest itself to people today. In other respects, however, it may appeal to them, since they are used to being more or less satisfied when they have once seen a work of art or a landscape, or have once listened to some scientific explanation. If such a matter is presented to them a second time, people today are apt to say: *Oh! I know that already. I have seen or heard that before!* Such is life in the abstract. In other domains in which life is judged according to what is to be found in it—according to its actuality—that is not the method of procedure. One does not often meet people for dinner who then excuse themselves from eating because they ate the day before. At meals, one repeats the same process over and over. Life is a constant repetition. If the spiritual is indeed to become real life to us—and unless it does, it cannot bring us into touch with the universal spiritual world—we must imitate in our souls the laws of life in the physical world, which world, although now grown torpid, was yet created by spirit. In particular, we shall become aware that a good deal is taking place in our soul if, with a certain rhythmic regularity, we allow such impressions to enter our souls as necessitate a certain freedom of thought, a certain emancipation from the mode of thought usual in the physical world.

The salvation (if we may use such a sentimental word) of human spiritual development depends on our not giving way in terms of spiritual things to the idle habit common today of saying:

Oh! I know that already, I have heard that before! Rather, we should take these matters as being like life itself, which is always connected with repetition, with what I might call the return of the same action at the same place. As soon as we are interested in letting our soul be permeated by the life of the spirit, our inner attention increases. It becomes so acute that we can grasp inwardly, in our soul, those important moments in which the connection with the spiritual world nearest to our heart can best be developed.

For instance, the moments of falling asleep and that of awaking are very important for the communion with the spiritual world. The moment of falling asleep would be less fruitful to most people at the beginning of their spiritual development, because immediately after one is asleep, one's consciousness is so dimmed that it cannot take in the spiritual. But the moment of passing from sleep into the waking state—if we only accustom ourselves not simply to let it pass by unobserved but to pay attention to it—may be very fruitful for us, if we try to wake up consciously while not allowing the outer world to approach us immediately with all its crude brutality. In this respect there is a great deal of good in the folk customs of ancient times, much that is quite right and today but little understood. Simple people who are not yet plastered over, so to speak, with intellectual culture, often say: *When you wake, you should not immediately look at the light*—that is, you should remain awhile in a state of wakefulness without allowing the brutal impressions of the outer world to press in on you immediately. If this be observed, it is possible at the moment of waking to see the dead who are karmically connected with us.

This is not the only time when they approach us, but it is then easiest to perceive them. At such a time we can see what takes place between the dead and us, both at the moment and beyond it; our perception of the spiritual world is not bound up with time as is the perception of the physical world. This in fact constitutes one of the difficulties of grasping of the spiritual world in its essence. At the moment of perception, something may momentarily reveal itself to us out of the spiritual world, something extending over a very great space of time. The difficulty is to have the spiritual presence of mind to grasp this far-reaching something at the moment, for that moment may (as is in fact generally the case) pass away *in status nascendi*. It is forgotten as soon as seen. That constitutes the great difficulty of grasping the spiritual world. Were it not for this, many, many people, especially today, would already be receiving impressions of the spiritual world.

In their normal state, people draw eighteen breaths per minute. This varies, because we breathe rather quicker during childhood and more slowly in old age. In general, however, it is correct to say that people draw eighteen breaths a minute. It is easy to reason that 18 times 60 make 1,080, the number of breaths per hour. Multiply this by 24 (the number of hours in a day) and you get 25,920 breaths in a day. Thus you see, my dear friends, that the same number regulates the human day of breathing as regulates the passage of the vernal point through the great cosmic year.

This is a sign that shows we are not just talking in a general, vague, and dimly mystical way when we say that the microcosm is an image of the macrocosm, but that human beings are actually governed in an important activity—upon which each moment of human life depends—by the same number and measure as the course of the Sun, in which course human beings themselves are placed.

Now let us consider something else. The so-called patriarchal age is seventy human years. Of course, seventy years is not a hard-and-fast rule for the duration of a human life; one may live much longer, because people are free beings and sometimes go beyond such limitations. We will however keep to this and say that the normal human life is seventy or seventy-one years, and let us see how many days these contain. Well, we have 365.25 days in a year. To begin with, we will multiply this number by 70 and get 25,567.5. Then we multiply this by 71 and get 25,932.75 days. This shows that between the ages of 70 and 71 comes the point of time when a person's life includes exactly 25,920 days—the patriarchal age. Thus, we have defined a human day by saying that it contains 25,920 breaths; we define the period of a human life by saying that it comes to 25,920 days.

[margin note: Pat. Age, ≈25,920 Days]

Now let us investigate something else that is not so difficult. We shall easily see that, if we divide the 25,920 years that the sun's vernal point requires to pass through the zodiac, by 365.25, the result is something like seventy or seventy-one. That means that if we consider the Platonic year as one great year and divide it till we bring out a day, we find the proportion of a day to a Platonic year.—What is that? It is the course of a human life. A man's life is to a Platonic year as a human day to a man's life.

The air is all around us; we breathe it in and breathe it out. According to the law of numbers, it is regulated so that when we have breathed in and out 25,920 times, our life is spent. What, then, is a day of our life? It is made up of our outgoing and incoming "I" and astral body, in and out of our physical and ether bodies. Thus, day after day the "I" and astral body leave and return, leave and come in, just like our breathing. Many of our friends will remember that to make this subject clear, in public lectures I have compared the alternation of waking and sleeping to deep breathing. Just as in breathing we breathe the air in and breathe out, so when we fall asleep and awake, the astral body and "I" go out and come in. This implies that a being exists, or can be presumed to exist, that breathes in and breathes out, just as we do in the eighteenth of a minute, and the breathing of this being signifies our outgoing and incoming astral body and "I." This being is none other than the living being of the Earth. As the Earth experiences day and night, it breathes; in the process of breathing, it bears our sleeping and awaking on its wings. It is the breathing process of a greater being.

[margin note: The Earth "breathes", it is the in and out of the astral & Ego]

Now let us consider the breathing process of an even greater being, the Sun in its orbit. Just as the Earth accomplishes a day by releasing and drawing in the "I" and astral body into human beings, likewise the great being corresponding to the Sun brings human beings forth. The seventy to seventy-one years are one day, as we have shown—one day of the Sun year, the great Platonic year. Our collective human life consists of breathing out and breathing in this great being, to whom is appointed the great Platonic year.

You see how it is; we draw one small breath in the eighteenth of a minute, which regulates our life; our life is lived on the Earth, the breathing of which comprises day and night, which corresponds with the outgoing and incoming "I" and astral body into our physical and etheric bodies. And we ourselves are breathed in by the great being whose life corresponds to the course of the Sun; our own life is one breath of this great being.

The 25,920 number... etc...

Now you see that as microcosms we are actually part of and subject to the same laws as are cosmic beings, just as the breath we draw is subject to our own human nature. Number and measure govern it. It is a great and wonderful thing. Its significance must cut deeply to our very hearts, that number and measure regulate the great cosmos, the macrocosm, exactly as they regulate us, the microcosm. This is not just a figure of speech; it is not merely mystically felt. The wisdom-filled contemplation of the world teaches us that as microcosms we stand within the macrocosm. When we make such simple calculations as these— which, of course, can be reached by the most ordinary scientific methods of reasoning—then, if our hearts are sensitive to the secrets of cosmic existence and not merely blocks of wood, the words *we have been placed into the universe* will no longer be an abstract statement. We will be fully alive to this fact. Knowing and a feeling will spring up within us, the fruits of which will be born in our will impulses, and our whole being will live in unison with the great life, divine cosmic existence.

This is the path along which, to some extent, we find our way into the spiritual world, the way that must be found at the time suggested in the previous lecture, when Christ will walk the Earth in his etheric form. I even indicated the very year in which he began to move etherically over the Earth—it must be found! However, people must accustom themselves to realizing the connection, the very intimate connection already being established from cosmic existence, which will, when it is felt and realized, bring about a need and intense longing to seek this union with the spiritual world. In any case, before very long, people will be compelled to realize one thing as follows.

When people are deadened by materialism, they may indeed deny the existence of a spiritual world, but they cannot fully kill in themselves the forces able to seek a connection with the spiritual world. People may delude themselves about the existence of a spiritual world, but they cannot kill the forces in their souls intended to bring them in touch with the spiritual world. This has very significant consequences, which should be considered especially today. Forces are present and they work, whether one believes in their existence or not. Materialists do not forbid the spiritually inclined forces in their souls to work; they cannot do so, and they do work. You may ask: Is it possible, then, for people to be materialists and yet to have forces at work within them that seek the spiritual? Yes, that is the case. Those forces are at work within them; regardless of what they may do, they work within them. What effect do those forces have? Wherever forces are present, their own original activity can be suppressed, but they then transform themselves into something else, into different forces.

You see, my dear friends, if we do not employ the spiritually tending forces to understand the spiritual world—I say only "understand," for only this is required at first—these forces will transform themselves into the forces of illusion in human life. Their activity then takes the form of inducing people to become subject to all kinds of illusion, illusions regarding the external world. It is not insignificant that this should be realized in our time, for never have people indulged their imagination as they do today, though they do not care for imagination, since their imagination works only along certain specific lines. If we needed to give examples of this, the fanciful weaving of those who wholly desire to be realists, materialists, light could be shed on all sorts of matters; there would be no end to it. We might perhaps begin, were it not heretical, by considering what politicians and public figures have prophesied a mere few weeks ago about the probable course of world events and what has occurred since, and we see that the capacities for illusion have played no small part for some years.

We might investigate many areas of life in the same way, and it is remarkable to note that everywhere we find these strongly developed capacities of illusion. Indeed they sometimes even lend a childlike (I might almost say a childish) character to the opinions and attitude to life of materialistically inclined people. When we see what is required today to make people understand one another or to make them see what is in front of their very nose, we can understand what I mean by "childlike" or even "childish."

Well, my dear friends, it is even so. When people turn away from the spiritual world, they must pay for it by becoming subject to illusion, by losing the capacity of forming accurate concepts of external physical reality and the course of events therein. They are then compelled to exercise their imagination in another direction, because they refuse to hold by the truth; whether the truth concerns the spiritual or the physical life, it comes to the same thing; they turn away from it. I once gave you an example that can be applied to this, for it is typical of it. There are plenty of discussions and arguments to be met as to the spiritual science I advocate.

Those who reason against spiritual science base their arguments on their own declaration that everything presented here is mere fantasy. "All of it has been imagined," they say, "and such flights of fancy cannot be taken seriously." Therefore, such people will not accompany us into the true spiritual world, because they believe it to be imaginary, and they despise such fanciful imaginations. Then they proceed to add all kinds of arguments that have no more to do with reality than black does to white. They they proceed (this is actually a typical example) to speak about my family descent and the way I did something or other in my life. They develop a bold imagination.

Here we can see, side by side, their turning away from the spiritual world and their capacity for illusion. Such people do not even notice this, yet they follow an absolute law. A certain amount of force in them tends toward the spiritual world, and a certain amount of force tends toward the physical world. If the force tending toward the spiritual world is not used for that purpose, it turns toward the physical world; not to study and grasp the truth and actuality there, but to drive people into illusions concerning life. This cannot be observed in each single case so that one can say, *Ah! This person has been driven into illusion by having turned away from the spiritual world.* We can certainly find such examples, but we have to look for them; they cannot be found immediately, because life is complicated and one person influences another. It is always the case that stronger souls influence the weaker, so that even when we find some such capacity for illusion in one person, it certainly may come from hatred toward or turning away from the spiritual world. Yet such dislike may not be in the soul of the deluded person but may have been suggested to that person. In spiritual areas, the danger of infection is infinitely greater than in any physical domain.

In our next lecture we shall consider how this is connected with general human karma. We shall consider how these matters—when observed in the light of the important law of the metamorphosis of the soul forces from the spiritual into forces of illusion—work in the whole connection of life and their connection with the conditions of development of our present time and those of the near future. We shall then carry further what we have begun today and connect it with the Christ and the mystery of the present age, thus shedding some light on the significance of the spiritual outlook in general.

THE HUMAN SOUL AND THE UNIVERSE, PART 1

Berlin, February 20, 1917

What we possess as the first fruit of spiritual science can, in its most practical and noble sense, lead us to feel that there is an inner human being within the ordinary person, who to the ordinary idea is really a second human being. In this respect, everyone consists in fact of two beings, one of which is composed more of our physical and ether bodies and belongs to the outer world—external in the sense that the physical body and, to some extent, the ether body are forms and images (or manifestations) of the divine spiritual beings that always surround us. In their true essence, our physical and etheric bodies are "I," though not as we initially know them—images neither of ourselves nor of our real being, but of the gods, whose whole existence is spent producing our physical and etheric bodies and bringing about their full development, just as we bring about the actions and deeds we accomplish.

The inner human is of such a nature that we are more closely related to the astral body and "I." To the universe, the astral body and "I" are younger than the physical and ether bodies. We know this from what is presented in the book *An Outline of Esoteric Science*. The physical body and ether body constitute what reposes, as it were, when we sleep and is readied for us by those divine spiritual beings that permeate the outer universe and make it manifest. The "I" and astral body, through the experiences, testing, and shifting that they undergo in the physical and etheric bodies, are to ascend gradually through the stages of development with which we have also become familiar.[1]

As I indicated in the previous lecture, we are connected with the universe, with the whole cosmos. This connection is such that (as I merely hinted in the previous lecture), it can even be calculated and expressed in numbers. Our connection with the universe can be expressed and shown in many other ways, of course, but I might say, to our great astonishment, that it can be expressed through the fact that the number of breaths we draw in a day equals the number of years needed for the vernal point to return to its original point of departure. These discoveries in the realm of numbers can, if we permeate them with feeling, fill us with awe—holy awe—when we reflect that we, too, belong to the divine spiritual universe manifested in all external phenomena.

The fact that we are the microcosm, the little world formed and manifested from the macrocosm, the great cosmos, is felt even more profoundly when we visualize facts that will be brought before our minds today, and that I may enumerate as follows: the three meetings of the human soul with the being of the universe. This is the subject about which I shall speak today.

We all know that, as earthly human beings, we bear within us the physical body and ether body, the astral body and "I." Each of the two beings I have mentioned bears inwardly what I might call two sub-beings. The more external human, the physical and ether body; the more inner human, the "I" and astral body. Now we know, moreover, that humankind is to develop further. The Earth as such will some day end. It will then evolve, through Jupiter, Venus, and Vulcan planetary evolution. Humankind during this time will rise stage by stage. As we know, a higher

---

1   See, for example, Rudolf Steiner, *The Stages of Higher Knowledge: Imagination, Inspiration, Intuition.*

being—the spirit self that will manifest inwardly—will be added to the human "I." This will reach full manifestation during the Jupiter evolution, which will follow that of our Earth. The life spirit will attain full manifestation in man during the Venus period; and the actual spirit body during the Vulcan period.

When, therefore, we look forward to the great cosmic future of humankind to these three stages of evolution, we look toward the spirit self, life spirit, and spirit body. But these three, which in a sense await us in our future evolution, are even now related to us in a certain sense, though they have not yet developed in the least; they are still enclosed in the bosom of the divine spiritual beings we have come to know as the higher hierarchies. They will come to us from the higher hierarchies, and today we already have a relationship with the higher hierarchies, which will endow us with spirit self, life spirit, and spirit body. Today, therefore, instead of using the more complicated expression and saying that we are in connection with the hierarchy of the angels, we can simply say that we are in connection with what will come to us in the future, our spirit self. Instead of saying that we are in connection with the archangels, we can say that we are in connection with what is to come to us in the future as our life spirit, and so on.

In the Christian sense, it makes no difference whether we place this being in the hierarchy of angels, or whether we refer to it in the older sense understood by the ancients when they spoke of their genius as the guiding human genius. We know that we live in a time when only few people (though this will soon change) can gaze into the spiritual world and perceive the things and the beings there. The time has passed when the beings, and even the various processes of evolution in the spiritual world, could be perceived in a much wider and more comprehensive sense; at the time when one spoke of the human genius, there was a direct, concrete perception of that being.

In a certain sense, we human beings are indeed already more than merely four-principled beings of physical, ether, and astral bodies and "I"-being, though only rudimentarily so at present (though in the spiritual world "rudimentary" is far more elevated than in the physical world). We already bear the seed of spirit self within us, as well as that of life spirit and spirit body; they will evolve from us in the future, though at present we have them only as seeds within us. This is not a mere abstract saying; it has concrete significance, because we have meetings—*real* meetings—with these higher principles of our being. Those meetings take place as follows.

As human beings, we would feel ourselves increasingly estranged from everything spiritual as time goes on—a condition very difficult to endure—if we did not occasionally encounter our spirit self. Our "I" must meet that higher self—the spirit self that we have yet to develop, and that in a spiritual sense is of like nature to the hierarchy of angels. Therefore, in simple language and speaking in the Christian sense, we may say that, from time to time, we must encounter a being of the angelic hierarchy, a being related closely to us; and when that being comes to us, it brings about a spiritual change in us that will enable us to receive a spirit self some day. We must also meet with a being of the archangelic hierarchy, because that being then affects us so that something is prepared that will one day lead to our development of life spirit.

In the recent past, this vision was still so strong that people could describe it quite concretely and objectively, describing it in terms now viewed as poetic fancies, though they were not intended as such. Plutarch therefore describes the relation of human beings to their genius, as follows—I would like to quote the passage literally.

Plutarch, the Roman writer, says that, in addition to the portion of the soul embedded in the earthly body, there is a purer part outside, soaring above the human head, appearing like a star, correctly called a person's *daemon*, who guides and whom the wise person willingly follows. In this concrete sense, Plutarch describes something he does not wish to be taken as a poetic fancy, but as a concrete external reality. Indeed, he describes it so concretely that he expressly states, "To a certain extent, the rest of the spiritual part of human beings can be perceived at the same time as the physical body, insomuch as it generally fills the same space; but the genius, the leading and guiding genius of humankind, is something separate that can be seen outside the head of every person."

Paracelsus, too, was one of the last who, without special training or gifts, could give forceful information about these things. He said very much the same from his own knowledge of this phenomenon. Many others said the same.

This genius is simply the spirit self in the process of evolving, though born by a being belonging to the angelic hierarchy. It is very important that we enter somewhat deeply into these matters; when this genius becomes perceptible, it has its own special conditions. This subject can also be considered from a very different point of view, but we will now look at it from this perspective. Let us consider the subject of an interaction between people, for we can learn much from this. It teaches us something that is certainly not without significance in the perception of the spiritual principles of the human being.

If we could observe the meeting of two people with only our physical sense of vision, we would notice merely that they come together, greet each other, and so on. But when we learn to observe such an event spiritually, we find that each time two people meet a spiritual process is established that, among other things, is also expressed outwardly by the fact that the part of their etheric bodies that forms the head becomes the expression of every feeling of sympathy and antipathy that those two individuals feel toward each other. And this continues as long as they are together.

Suppose two people were to meet who cannot stand each other; an extreme case, but there are such in life. Suppose two individuals meet who dislike each other, and that this feeling of antipathy is mutual. It can then be seen that the part of the ether body that forms the head projects beyond the head in both cases, and that both the etheric heads incline toward each other. A mutual antipathy between persons meeting is expressed as a continual bowing and inclining of the etheric head of each toward the other. When two persons come together who love each other, a similar process can be observed; but here the etheric head inclines back, it bends backward. Now whether the etheric head bends forward as though in greeting when antipathy is felt, or bends back where love is felt, in both cases the physical head then becomes freer than usual. This is of course always relative; the ether body does not emerge entirely but extends in length, so that a continuation can be seen. A more rarefied than normal ether body then fills the physical body, with the result that, by reason of the exceptional transparency of the ether body, the astral body still inside the head becomes more clearly visible to clairvoyant vision. Thus, not only is there a movement of the ether body, but also an alteration in the astral light of the head.

This then, my dear friends, is no poetic imagination but an actual fact and the reason, in places where such things are understood, why people who are capable of selfless love are represented with an aura around their heads, also known as a halo. When two people meet, with only a strong tinge of egoism in their love, this phenomenon is not as apparent. But when people come into contact with others at certain times when they are not so concerned with themselves and their personal relation to another, but are filled with a universal human love for all humanity, such phenomena appear. At such times, the astral body in the area of the head becomes clearly visible. If there are people present then who are able to see this clairvoyantly in a person, they can see the halo and must paint or otherwise represent it as reality. These matters are absolutely in keeping with the objective facts of the spiritual world; but what is thus objectively present and a lasting reality in human evolution is connected with something else.

As human beings, we must necessarily from time to time enter inner communion with our spirit self, the spirit self visible in the astral aura in rudimentary form as I described. But it must still be developed; it will be radiated down, as it were, from above, and flow in from the future. Human beings must occasionally be brought into touch with the spirit self.

When does this happen? We now come to the first meeting about which we must speak. When does it take place? It happens quite simply in normal sleep, on almost every occasion between sleeping and waking. With simple country people, who are closer to the life of nature, and who go to bed with the setting Sun and get up at sunrise, this meeting takes place in the middle of their time of sleeping, which is usually the middle of the night. With those who have detached themselves from connections with nature, this is not so much the case. However, this depends on human free will. People of modern culture can regulate their lives as they please, and though this fact is bound to affect their lives, they can still regulate it as they please within certain limits. Nonetheless, they, too, can experience in the middle of a long sleep what may be called an inner union with the spirit self—that is, with the spiritual qualities from which the spirit self will be extracted. They can have a meeting with their genius. Thus, this meeting with one's genius takes place every night during every period of sleep, though this must not be taken too literally.

This meeting is important for human beings. All the feelings that gladden the soul with respect to its connection with the spiritual world proceed from this meeting with our genius during sleep. The feeling of our connection with the spiritual world, which we may have in our waking state, is an effect of this meeting with our genius. That is the first meeting with the higher world, and it may be said that most people are initially unaware of it, though they will become increasingly conscious as they realize its effects by refining their waking conscious life, through absorbing the ideas and concepts of spiritual science, until their souls become refined enough to observe carefully these aftereffects. It all depends on whether the soul is refined enough, sufficiently acquainted with its inner life to be able to observe these.

This meeting with the genius is brought to the consciousness of everyone in some form or other, but the present day materialism that fills the mind with ideas from the materialistic view of the world and especially the life of today, permeated as it is by materialistic opinions, prevent the soul from noticing the results of the meeting. As people gradually fill their minds with more spiritual ideas than those presented by materialism, the perception of the nightly meeting with the genius will become increasingly self-evident.

The second meeting we must discuss is higher. From the indications given, one may gather that the first meeting with the genius is connected with the course of the day. If we had not, through modern civilization, become free to adjust our lives according to our own convenience, this meeting would take place at the hour of midnight. People would meet their genius every night at midnight. But because of the exercise of human free will, the time of this meeting has become flexible; the hour when the "I" meets the genius is no longer fixed. The second meeting, however, is not as flexible; what is more connected with the astral body and ether body is not so apt to move from its place in the cosmic order. What is connected with the "I" and the physical body is greatly displaced in modern human beings. The second meeting is already more connected with the great macrocosmic order. Even as the first meeting is connected with the course of the day, the second is connected with the course of the year.

Here, I must call attention to various matters I have already indicated in this connection from another point of view. A human life in its entirety does not run its course quite evenly through the year. When the Sun develops its greatest heat, human beings depend far more on their own physical life and the surrounding physical life than in the winter, when they must struggle, in a sense, with the outer phenomena of the elements, and are thrown back more on themselves. However, then their spiritual nature is freer, and they are more connected with the spiritual world—both their own and that of the Earth—with the whole spiritual environment.

Thus, the peculiar sentiment we connect with the mystery of Christmas and its festival is in no way arbitrary, but hangs together with the fixing of the Christmas festival. At the time during winter appointed for that festival, people, as does the whole Earth, surrender themselves to the spirit. They then pass through a realm, as it were, in which the spirit is near. The result is that around Christmas time and through our present New Year, people experience a meeting of their astral body with the life spirit, just as they experience the first meeting, that of one's "I" with the spirit self. The nearness of Jesus Christ depends on this meeting with the life spirit. Jesus Christ reveals himself through the life spirit. He reveals himself through a being of the realm of the archangels. He is, of course, an immeasurably higher being than they are, but that is not the point at the moment; what we have to consider is that Jesus Christ reveals himself through a being of the archangelic order. Thus through this meeting we draw especially near to Jesus Christ at the present stage of development (which has existed since the Mystery of Golgotha) and, in a certain sense, we may call the meeting with the life spirit the meeting with Jesus Christ in the very depths of our soul.

When people have thus deepened and spiritualized their life of impressions and feelings—either through developing spiritual consciousness in the realm of religious meditation or exercises or, to supplement these, have accepted the concepts and ideas of spiritual science—then, just as they can experience the effects of the meeting with their spirit self during waking life, likewise they will also experience the effects of the meeting with the life spirit, or Christ. It is a fact, my dear friends that, immediately after Christmas and up to Easter, conditions are particularly favorable for bringing this meeting with Jesus Christ to our consciousness. In a profound sense—and this should not be blotted out by today's abstract materialistic culture—the Christmas season is connected with processes taking place in the Earth, because human beings together with the Earth participate in the Christmas changes in the Earth.

Processes in the heavens determine the Easter season. Easter Sunday is fixed for the first Sunday after the first full moon after the vernal equinox. Thus, whereas Christmas is fixed by the conditions of the Earth, Easter is determined from above. Just as we (through all that was described) are connected with the conditions of the Earth, similarly are we connected, through what I will now describe, with the conditions of the heavens, the great cosmic conditions.

Easter is the season of the year when everything aroused in us by the meeting with Christ at Christmas actually unites with our physical, earthly human nature. The great Mystery that now brings the Mystery of Golgotha home to us during the Easter season (the Good Friday mystery) signifies, among other things, that the Christ, who has been moving as it were beside us during this season draws even closer to us. In fact, roughly speaking, he disappears into us in a sense and permeates us so that he can remain with us during the season that follows the Mystery of Golgotha (the summer season), during which people in the ancient mysteries tried to unite themselves with John in a way not possible after the Mystery of Golgotha.

As we see, in this sense we are the microcosm, and we are attached to the macrocosm in a profound way. There is a continual union with the macrocosm in annual seasons, and this union, being a more inner process in us, is related to the course of the year. Therefore, spiritual science gradually endeavors to reveal the ideas, the spiritually scientific concepts, that humankind may acquire about the way Christ is able now to penetrate and permeate our earthly life since the Mystery of Golgotha.

At this point, I feel compelled to make an important interpolation that should be thoroughly understood, particularly by friends of spiritual science. It should never be claimed that our attempts at spiritual science are a substitute for the life and exercise of religion. Spiritual science may be taken as a support, as a foundation for the life and exercise of religion in the highest sense, and particularly in relation to the mystery of the Christ, but it should not be made into a religion. We should be clear that religion in its living form and practice kindles the spiritual consciousness of the human community.

If this spiritual consciousness is to become a living thing in human beings, we cannot possibly remain at a standstill, settling for merely abstract ideas of God or Christ; we must stand renewed amid the religious practices and activities (which may take different forms in various people) as something that provides people with a religious center and appeals to them as such. If this religious sentiment is deep enough and finds a means of stimulating the soul, it will soon feel a longing—a real longing—for the very ideas that can be developed in spiritual science. If spiritual science may be said to be a support for a religious life, as it certainly is, objectively speaking, subjectively the time has come when we may say that those with true religious feelings are driven by those feelings to seek knowledge. Spiritual consciousness is acquired through religious feeling, and spiritual knowledge through spiritual science, just as knowledge of nature is acquired through natural science. Spiritual consciousness leads to an impulse to acquire spiritual knowledge. It may be said that today an inner religious life may subjectively drive people to spiritual science.

The third meeting takes place when people approach the spirit body, which will be developed only in the far future and is brought to us by a being of the hierarchy of the Archai. We may say that the ancients were sensitive to this, as are even the people of today, though the latter are no longer conscious of the deeper truth of the subject when speaking of such matters. The ancients experienced this encounter as a meeting with what permeates the world and that we can now barely distinguish in ourselves or the world, but in which we merge in the world as in a unity. Just as we can speak of the second as a meeting with Jesus Christ, likewise can we speak of the third as a meeting with the Father

[handwritten margin note: 3rd Mtg]

[handwritten note at bottom: a meeting c̄ The Father Principle]

Principle, the Father, with what lies at the world foundation, which we experience if we have the right feeling for "the Father" as meant by the various religions.

This meeting is of such that it reveals our intimate connection with the macrocosm, the divine spiritual universe. The daily course of universal, world processes includes a meeting with our genius; the yearly course includes our meeting with Jesus Christ; and the course of a whole human life, of this human life, my dear friends—which normally can be described as the human life of seventy years—includes the meeting with the Father Principle. For a certain time, our physical earthly life is prepared, and rightly so, by education (largely unconsciously today, yet it is prepared), and between the ages of twenty-eight and forty-two, most people experience the meeting with the Father Principle unconsciously—and although unconsciously, nonetheless fully appreciated in the soul's intimate depths. The effects of this may extend into later life if we develop fine perceptions sufficiently to note what thus comes into our life from within ourselves as the result of our meeting with the Father Principle.

During a certain period of our life (that of preparation), education should make the experience of meeting with the Father Principle as deep as possible. This can be done in many different ways. One way is to arouse people during their years of schooling with a strong feeling for the glory of the world, its greatness, and the sublime nature of world processes.

We withhold a great deal from growing boys and girls when we fail to show them all the revelations of beauty and greatness in the world, because then, instead of having a devoted reverence and respect for these, they may pass by them without seeing. When we fill the minds of young people with thoughts that connect their heart feelings with the beauty and greatness of the world, we prepare them for the right meeting with the Father Principle.

This meeting is of great significance for the life between death and a new birth. This meeting with the Father Principle, which normally occurs between the ages of twenty-eight and forty-two, can be a strong force and support to people when they must, as we know, recapitulate their earthly life retrospectively after having passed through the portals of death and as they pass through the soul world. This retrospective journey— which lasts one-third as long as the time lived between birth and death, as we know—can be made strong and forceful, as indeed it should be if people can see themselves at a certain point and place meeting with the being whom they can only dimly guess at and express in clumsy words when speaking of the Father of the cosmic order. This is an important image that, after we have passed through the gates of death, should always be present with us, along with the picture of death itself.

Thus, my dear friends, because the truths of spiritual science concerning human life as a whole affect our life so deeply, they are indeed serious in especially important situations. Such truths can provide serious explanations of life, which we need in an age when we must find our way out of the materialism that rules today's world order and point of view, insofar as these depend on us. Stronger forces will be needed to overcome the strong connection with the purely material powers that rule human beings today and to give people again the possibility of recognizing their connection with the spiritual world through the direct experiences of life.

It is natural that a certain question should arise in connection with this. There are those who die before they reach midlife, when they would normally meet the Father Principle. We must consider the cases of those whose death is caused by some external means, such as illness (which is outer) or some weakness. If, through such an early death the meeting with the Father Principle has not yet occurred in the subconscious depths of the soul, it will instead take place at the hour of death; the meeting occurs at the moment of death.

Here, we may express, somewhat differently, what actually has expressed already in another form and in a similar connection

in the book *Theosophy*, referring to the always deplorable phenomenon of bringing one's own life to an end by one's own will.[2]
People would never do this if they could only see the significance
of this act. Once spiritual science has been taken truly into people's feelings and thoughts, there will be no more suicides. The
meeting with the Father Principle at the hour of death, when
death occurs before midlife, depends on death that comes from
outside, not a death brought about by oneself. The difficulty
then encountered by the soul, which is described from another
perspective in *Theosophy*, might be described from what we are
saying today; we might say that, through a person's self-chosen
death, one may eventually deprive oneself of meeting with the
Father Principle in this incarnation.

If we speak in a more abstract way about the beings of the
higher hierarchies, we can speak in a more concrete way of the
fact that man himself—in the experiences at first passed through
unconsciously, but which even during his life between birth and
death may be brought to his consciousness—may ascend in three
stages: through the meeting with his genius, through the meeting
with Jesus Christ, and through the meeting with the Father.

Of course, much depends on gaining as many concepts as
possible that force their way into our feelings—concepts that
refine our inner soul life so that we do not pass things by care-
lessly and inattentively, which, in reality, if we are only attentive,
play a part in our lives. In this respect, education will have a
great deal to do in the near future. I would just like to present
one such concept. Just think how life would be infinitely deepened if such details concerning karma could be added to the
general knowledge, such as the fact that, when a life comes to an
end in early youth, the meeting with the Father Principle occurs
at the hour of death. This shows that the particular karma of
this person made an early death necessary, so that an exceptional meeting with the Father Principle must occur.

---

2   See Rudolf Steiner, *Theosophy*, pp. 118–119.

What actually occurs in such a case? Such a person is destroyed from without—one's physical being is undermined from without. In illness, too, this is actually the case. The scene of this meeting with the Father Principle is really here on the physical Earth. When it happens that this external physical Earth has destroyed a person, the meeting with the Father Principle can be seen at that very place, and of course it is always to be seen again in retrospect. This, however, makes it possible for a person, throughout the whole of one's life after death, to hold firmly the thought of the place on Earth where, descending from heavenly heights, the Father Principle came to the meeting that then took place. Recollection of this makes one want to be as active as possible to work down into the physical Earth from the spiritual world.

Now, if we consider our present time from this perspective and try to arouse the same feeling of solemnity as we have just tried to do with the meeting with the Father Principle—trying not merely to view the many premature deaths now occurring in the light of feeling or abstract concept—we will be forced to acknowledge that these were predestined in preparation of the coming need for a great activity to be directed from the spiritual world to the physical Earth.

This is another aspect of what I have said often in reference to the tragic events of the last few years: those who pass so early through the portals of death today will become special helpers in the future development of humanity, which will indeed require strong forces to disentangle itself from materialism. But all this must be brought to human consciousness; it *must not* occur unconsciously. Therefore, it is necessary even now for souls here on the Earth to make themselves receptive (I have already mentioned this), otherwise the forces developed in the spiritual world may go in other directions. So that these forces—these predestined forces—may become fruitful to the Earth, it is necessary that there should be souls on the Earth permeated with the knowledge of the spiritual world. And there must increasingly be more such souls on Earth. Let us therefore try to make the content of spiritual science fruitful, which must be presented first in words. Through the aid of language (I mentioned this in the first lecture), the language we learn through spiritual science, let us try to reanimate the old concepts that are, not without purpose, interwoven in our present life. Let us try to re-enliven what we have heard from Plutarch—that human beings, even physically, are permeated by the spiritual human being, and that in a peculiar though normal way, people have a higher spiritual principle outside their head that represents one's genius and that, if they are wise, they obey. Try, as I said, to take the feelings acquired by spiritual science to our assistance—so that the phenomena of life does not pass us by unnoticed.

In conclusion, we will take one feeling today, one concept, that may be of great help to our souls. Unfortunately, many in our modern materialistic age find it very difficult to feel what I might call "the holiness of sleep." Materialistic life is being somewhat softened by this period of trial, and not only should it thus remain softened—which we can hardly hope for if materialism remains as strong as it is; rather, it should become even more softened. It is indeed a strange phenomenon of human intelligence today that people are entirely devoid of respect for the holiness of sleep. We need only consider how many people who spend their evening hours in purely materialistic ways, going to sleep without developing the realization (which in fact can never become a living thing in a materialistic mind) that sleep unites us with the spiritual world, that sleep sends us across into the spiritual world. These matters are not mentioned to blame, nor to drive people into asceticism; we must live with the world, but we must also open our eyes; only in this way can we wrench our bodily nature away from the lower and lift it higher. People should at least gradually become able to develop a feeling that can be expressed somewhat as follows: "I am going to sleep; until I awake, my soul will be in the spiritual world. There it will meet with the guiding power of my earthly life, who lives in the spiritual world, and who soars round and surrounds my head. My soul will meet with my genius. The wings of my genius will come in contact with my soul."

Yes, my dear friends, in terms of overcoming materialistic life, a great deal, a very great deal, depends on whether people can create a strong feeling of what this means when considering their relation to sleep. Materialistic life can be overcome only by stimulating intimate feelings such as these, which are themselves in correspondence with the spiritual world. Only when we intensify and activate such feelings will the life of sleep become so intense that contact with the spiritual world will gradually be able to strengthen our waking life, as well. We will then have not merely the sensory world around us, but also the spiritual world, which is the true, the truly real, world. This world that we generally call the "real" one, as I discussed in the previous open lecture, is nothing but a reflection, or image, of the actual real one. The real world is the world of spirit. The small community devoted to Anthroposophy, or spiritual science, today will be better able to grasp the earnest signs of the times and undergo the severe trials of today if, in addition to all the other trials to which we are subjected today, it learns to consider this a time of trial, of testing and probation, whether we are, with sufficient strength of soul and warmth of heart, able to unite our whole being with the spiritual science that we must absorb through our reason and intellect.

With these words, I wanted to emphasize again what I have often said here before—that spiritual science will not find its right place in human hearts until it is no longer merely a theory and knowledge but when, symbolically, it continually permeates and penetrates the soul, just as our physical blood, our heart's blood, constantly permeates and gives life to our physical nature.

MORALITY AS A
GERMINATING FORCE

Berlin, February 27, 1917

In our previous lecture, I spoke to you about the human soul's three meetings with the regions related to the spiritual world. I will have to say a few more things about these, which will give me an opportunity to answer a question following the previous public lecture in the Architectural Hall regarding the forces that bring one's karma, or outer destiny, from a former incarnation. I have been told that this is very difficult to understand. In these lectures, I will return to this subject, but it is preferable to do so after having discussed a few points that may perhaps help make the question better understood. Today, however, to make the question of the three meetings with the spiritual world even clearer, by way of episode, I plan to insert something that it seems to me important to discuss just now.

When we consider the ideas and concepts that have found their way into human souls of all educational levels as a result of the spiritual development during the last century, we see how strongly its influence tended to lead people to consider world evolution and the human being's place in it—solely according to the standard of natural science and its ideas. There are, of course, plenty of people still living today who do not believe their attitude of mind and soul has been formed by natural-scientific concepts. Such people do not, however, see the deeper bases upon which their minds were formed; they do not know that the ideas of natural science have just slipped in a one-sided way, not only determining their thoughts but even their feelings in a certain way. People today who reflect along the lines laid down for everyone in conventional centers of education, whose mind and disposition have been formed according to them, and whose ideas are based on what is taught there, cannot possibly feel the true connection between what we call the world of morality, or moral feeling, and the world of outer phenomena. If we ponder, according to the ideas of our times, the way the Earth, and indeed the whole firmament, is supposed to have developed and may come to its final end, we think along the lines of purely outer, sensory perceptible facts. Just consider the deep significance to human souls concerning the existence of the so-called Kant-Laplace theory of world creation, according to which the Earth and the whole heavens arose from a purely material cosmic mist (it is in fact represented as purely material), and were then formed according to purely earthly physical and chemical laws, developed further according to these laws, and, so it is believed, will also end through those same laws. A condition will some day come about in which the whole world will mechanically end, just as it came into being.

Of course, as I have said before, there are those today who do not allow themselves to think of it in this way. That, however, is not the point; it is not the ideas we form that signify, but the attitude of mind that gives rise to those ideas. The concept to which I have just alluded is purely materialistic—one about which Hermann Grimm says a piece of carrion that a hungry dog circles around is a more attractive sight than the construction of the world according to the Kant-Laplace theory. Yet it arose and developed. One may even say that, to the great majority of those who study it, the idea even seems illuminating. There are few who, like Hermann Grimm, ask how future generations will be able to account for the arising of this mad idea in our age; they will wonder how such a delusion could ever have seemed illuminating to so many.

There are only a few who have the soundness of mind to put the question this way, and those who do are simply considered more or less wrongheaded. But, as I said, the point is not so much the ideas themselves as the impulse and frame of mind that made them possible. Such concepts arose because of certain mental attitudes. Yet, though they came from educated people and were given out by them, most still believe that the world did not originate in any such mechanical impulse, but that divine impulses must have played a part in its creation. Nonetheless, it remains a fact that such concepts were possible. It was possible for human mental attitudes and soul dispositions to form in such a way that a purely mechanical idea about the origin of the world was conceived.

This shows that, at the bottom of human souls, there is a tendency to form concepts of a materialistic nature. This tendency is not found only among the uneducated and others who believe in this idea; it exists in the broadest circles among all kinds of people, yet most people today are still rather shy about following Haeckel, picturing everything spiritual in a material form. They lack the necessary courage for this. They still acknowledge something spiritual, but do not give the matter further thought. If the mentioned concept holds, there can then be room only for the spiritual, and especially for the moral, in a certain sense.

Just consider; if the world really came into being as the Kant-Laplace theory proposes, and comes to its end only through physical forces, dragging all humankind to the grave with it, along with all their ideas, feelings, and will impulses, what then, apart from all else, would become of the whole moral order of the world? Suppose for a moment that the condition of the burial of all things came to pass. What good would it have been ever to have pronounced some things good and others evil? What would it avail to say this is right and that is wrong? These would be only forgotten ethical concepts, swept away as something that, if this idea of the world order were correct, might not survive in even a single soul. In fact, the matter would stand thus: from purely mechanical causes, by physical and possibly chemical forces, the world came into being, and by like means it will come to an end. By means of these forces phenomena appear like bubbles, produced by humankind. Among human beings themselves the moral ideas of right and wrong, good and evil arise; but the whole world passes into the stillness of the grave. All right and wrong, good and evil, is merely a human illusion, forgotten and vanishing when the world becomes "the grave." Thus, the only thing that stands for the moral world order is the feeling people have as long as the episode lasts, which extends from the first state to the last—that people require such ideas for their common life; that people must form these moral ideals, though they can never take root in a purely mechanical world order.

The forces of nature (heat, electricity, and so on) intervene in the plan of nature, where they make themselves felt. However, if the mechanical plan of the world were correct, the force of morality would exist only in the human mind; it would not intervene in the natural order. It would not be like heat that expands bodies, or like light that illumines them, makes them visible, and permeates the realm of space. This moral force is present and soars as a great illusion over the mechanical world order. And it vanishes, dissolves away, when the world is transformed into the grave.

People do not carry these thoughts sufficiently to their logical conclusion; hence, they are not on guard against a mechanical world order, but allow it to remain—not from kindness of heart, but from laziness. If they have a certain want in their hearts, they simply say that science does not require us to think deeply about this mechanical world order; faith demands something else of us, so we put our faith side-by-side with science and simply believe in something more than mechanical nature; we just believe what a certain inner demand of our hearts compels. That is very convenient! There is no need, therefore, to rebel against what Herman Grimm, for instance, felt to be a mad idea of modern science. No rebellion is needed. But those who really wish to think their thoughts through to their conclusion cannot justify this attitude.

One may ask: Why do people today live blindly in such an impossible position, making it impossible to think logically? Why do people accept such a position? As strange as this may sound to one who is unfamiliar with such thought and hears it for the first time, the reason is that people have more or less forgotten during the course of the last century how to think truly of the Christ Mystery, which must take its place at the very center of the life of the age. People have forgotten how to think of it in its actual, true sense. The way that people think of the Christ Mystery in recent times should be such that it radiates into their entire thinking and feeling. The position human beings have assumed toward the Christ since the Mystery of Golgotha represents the standard of their collective ideas and sentiments. I may have more to say about this in the near future. If people cannot view the Mystery of Christ as a true reality, they are also unable to develop ideas and concepts by which to gauge the worldviews of others, ideas permeated by reality and actually capable of penetrating the truth.

This is what I wanted above all to make clear to you today. If people really think as I have just illustrated, as most people of the present day do, whether consciously or not, the world is then divided into a *mechanical* natural order on the one hand, and on the other into a *moral* world order. Now, to timid souls, who often believe themselves to be very courageous, the Christ Mystery forms part of the purely moral world order. This applies mainly to those who see no more in the Christ Mystery than the fact that at a particular time a great, perhaps even the greatest, teacher of the Earth appeared, and that his teaching is the most important thing. Now, if Christ is considered only to be the greatest teacher of humanity, this view is quite compatible in a sense with the twofold division of the world into a natural order and a moral order. Of course, even if the Earth had formed itself into the mechanical world order as represented, eventually becoming the common grave of all things, it might still be possible for a great teacher to arise who might accomplish much to make human beings better and to convert them. His teachings might have been sublime, but they would avail nothing when, at the end of all things, everything becomes a grave and even Christ's teachings would have disappeared, leaving not even a remembrance of him in any living being. People do not like to think this, but their dislike would not alter the fact. If it is desired to believe absolutely in a merely mechanical world order, it would be impossible to avoid such thoughts as these.

Everything depends on realizing the fact that something was accomplished in the Mystery of Golgotha that does not belong merely to the moral world order, but also to the whole collective cosmic order; something that belongs not only to the moral reality—which according to the mechanical world order must be nonexistent—but also to the whole intensive reality. We will be able to grasp what is really in question by turning our thoughts again to the three meetings I mentioned in the previous lecture, taking them in a different sense from that to which I then referred.

I do not wish to leave a vague impression in your minds about this, so I will say at once that in the sleeping state, the next incarnation is as the knowledge of the next day. We know from experience that when tomorrow comes the Sun will rise, and we know more or less how it will run its course, although we may not know tomorrow's weather or what separate events may affect our lives. Likewise, the soul is a prophet during our sleep, but a prophet who knows only of what is great and cosmic; not about the weather. If we suppose that, during sleep, the soul becomes aware of the details of the next incarnation, we would be making the same mistake as those who think that because they know that next Sunday the Sun will surely rise and set, as well as certain universal facts, they could therefore predict the weather. This does not change the fact that while we are asleep we do have to concern ourselves with the future. We are met during time of sleep by those forces whose nature is like our spirit self and work on forming our future.

I told you that every time we sleep, in the intermediate state between going to sleep and waking, we meet beings of the spiritual world, beings of a like nature to our spirit self (as we are accustomed to call it), beings of the same substance and kind. This means that when we awake from sleep, we have had a meeting with a spiritual being, and though we may be quite unaware of having had this experience, we nevertheless carry the effects into our outer physical lives. What takes place in our soul during this daily meeting is in a certain way connected with the future of humankind. People of today, unless they occupy themselves with spiritual science, know very little as yet of what takes place in the depth of their souls during sleep. Dreams, which in ordinary life betray something of this, do indeed reveal something, but they reveal it in such a way that the truth does not come easily to light. When we awake in a dream or out of a dream, or remember a dream, this is connected mostly with ideas we already acquired in life, or reminiscences. These are, however, only the garments of what really lives in the dream or during sleep. When our dreams clothe themselves in pictures from our daily life, they are merely the garments; dreams reveal what actually takes place in the soul during sleep, and that is related neither to the past nor to the present, but to the future.

In sleep the forces are found that, in a human being, can be compared to the germinal forces that develop in the plant for the production of a new one. As the plant grows it always develops the germinal forces for the new plant in the following year. Those forces reach their peak in forming the seed, in which they become visible. However, as a plant grows, while it is growing, the seed forces for the next plant are already present. Likewise, the germinal forces—whether for the next incarnation or even for the Jupiter period—are present in human beings, and we form these mainly during sleep. The forces then formed, my dear friends, are not related immediately to individual experiences, but to the basic forces of the next incarnation: they relate to the forces of the next incarnation. In sleep, we work on our seeds for our next incarnation into the future. So that while we are asleep, we already live in the future.

Another, further meeting (if I leave out the second) is the third meeting, which I said in the last lecture takes place only once during a person's lifetime, in midlife. I said that when people are in their thirties, they encounter what might be called the Father Principle, whereas we meet the Spirit Principle every night. This meeting with the Father Principle is of very great significance, because it must happen. You will recall that I explained, even those who die before the age of thirty have this experience, but if they live through their thirties it comes in the course of life, whereas in the case of premature death it occurs sooner. You know that, as the result of that meeting, people become able to impress the experiences of the present life so deeply into themselves that those experiences can work into the next incarnation. Thus, the meeting with the Father Principle is connected with the earthly life of the next incarnation, while our meeting with the Spirit Principle is for the whole future; it radiates over the whole of our future life, as well as over the life experienced between birth and a new birth.

The laws with which this meeting (which we experience only once in a life) are interwoven do not pertain to the Earth. They are laws that have remained in the Earth's evolution, just as they were at the time of the Moon evolution. On the physical side, they are connected with our physical descent and everything that physical heredity signifies. This physical heredity is indeed only one side of the matter; there are spiritual laws behind it, as I have explained. Thus, everything that happens regarding the meeting with the Father Principle points back to the past; it is the legacy of the past. It points back to the Moon evolution and to earlier incarnations, while what takes place during sleep points toward the future. Just as what takes place during sleep forms the seed for the future, what comes about as a result of people being born as the descendants of their ancestors—carrying from former incarnations what is necessary should be brought over—all that has remained from the past.

Both what relates to the future and to the past are, in a sense, striving outside the natural order. The peasant still goes to sleep at sunset and rises at dawn; but people progress in so-called civilization, they break away from the natural order. One meets people in cities (though they may not be very numerous) who go to bed in the morning and arise at night. Human beings are freeing themselves from the mere order of nature; the development of their free will makes it possible to do so.

In a sense, therefore, because we are preparing for a future that is not yet here, we are torn away from the natural order. When we carry the past into the present, especially the past connected with the Moon, we are also torn loose from the order of nature. No one can prove, according to the universal laws of nature, the necessity that John Smith should be born in 1914; such an event is not ruled by necessity, as is the rising of the Sun or other natural occurrences, but by the natural order of the Moon. During the Moon period, everything was like the order of our birth on Earth.

Human beings, however, are subject entirely to the natural order in regard to what has immediate significance to the present, our earthly existence. In the case of the Father Principle, we bear the past within us; with regard to the Spirit Principle, the future—in terms of the meeting, which I said occurs in the course of the year and is now connected with meeting Christ—we are connected with the natural order. If we were not, Christmas might be celebrated by one person in December and by another in March, and so on. However, although different nations have different designations for the festival of Christmas, there is some kind of festivity everywhere in late December that always bears some relation to the meeting I discussed. Thus, with this meeting that is inserted into the course of the year, people (for the very reason that this is their present) are in direct connection with the order of nature. However, with respect to the past and the future, we have become free from it, and, indeed, have been free from it for thousands of years.

In ancient times, humankind joined in the natural order in terms of both past and future. Germanic countries in antiquity, for instance, regulated birth according to the natural order. Birth, which was regulated by the mysteries, might take place only at a set time of the year. Thus, it was inserted into the natural order. In antiquity, long before the Christian era, conception and birth were regulated in the Germanic countries by what is only faintly preserved in the myth of worshipping Hertha [the Mother Earth Goddess]. In those days, her worship was no less than this: when Hertha descended in her chariot and approached humanity, it was the time of conception. After she withdrew, this might no longer take place. This was strictly obeyed, to the degree that anyone not born within the appointed season was thought to lack honor, because that person's human existence was not in harmony with the natural order. In ancient times, birth and conception were adapted to the course of nature just as much as sleeping and waking were. In those days, people slept when the Sun had set and woke at dawn. These practices have become displaced, but the central event adapted to the course of the year cannot be displaced. By means of this, through its harmony with the order of nature, something is retained and must be so retained in the human soul.

What then is the whole purpose of humanity's earthly evolution? That human beings should adapt to the Earth and take the Earth conditions into themselves; that they should carry into their future evolution what the Earth has been able to give to them, not in just a single incarnation, but in the whole of their incarnations on Earth.

This then is the purpose of the Earth evolution. This purpose, however, can be fulfilled only if, during their sojourn on Earth, human beings forget to some degree their connection to cosmic and heavenly powers. And human beings have learned to do this.

We know, in fact, that in antiquity human beings possessed atavistic clairvoyance, and could work into that heavenly powers. Human beings were still connected with them; the kingdom of heaven in a sense extended into the human heart. This had to change so that human beings could develop free will. To become connected to Earth, human beings could no longer retain the kingdom of heaven in their vision, or direct perception.

However, this is why (at the time of humanity's closest connection to the Earth, during the fifth epoch in which we now live) humankind has became materialistic. Materialism is only the most complete, the most extreme expression of humankind's relation to the Earth, and if nothing else had happened this would have brought about our complete and utter subjection to the Earth. We would have had to become related to it and gradually share in its destiny; we would have had to follow the same path as the Earth herself pursues; we would have dovetailed entirely into the Earth's evolution—unless something else occurred. Human beings, together with the Earth, would have had to tear themselves away, as it were, from the cosmos, uniting their destiny completely with that of the Earth. However, that was not the plan for humanity; something else was intended. Human beings had to unite in the proper way with the Earth, on the one hand; on the other, although they had to become related to the Earth through their nature, nonetheless messages would descend to them from the spiritual world that would lift them above the Earth again. This descent of the heavenly message came about through the Mystery of Golgotha. Therefore the being who went through the Mystery of Golgotha had to assume human nature as well as the nature of a heavenly being.

This means that we must think of Jesus Christ not only as one who, although the highest, entered human evolution and developed within it, but also as one who possessed a heavenly nature, who not only taught and propagated doctrine but also brought to the Earth something from Heaven. This is why it is important to understand the true nature of the Baptism in Jordan. It is not merely a moral action. I am not saying that it is not a moral action, but that it is more than that; it is also an actual deed. Something took place then that is just as real as natural events. If I warm something by some means of heating, the warmth passes into the thing that is warmed. Likewise, the Christ being passed into Jesus of Nazareth at the Baptism by John. That is certainly a moral act in the highest degree, but it is also a reality in the course of nature, just as real as natural phenomena. The important thing is that we should understand that this is not something that originates in rationalistic concepts, which always accord only with mechanical, physical, or chemical nature; rather, it is something that, as idea, is just as much an actual fact as are the laws of nature, or indeed the forces of nature. Once this is grasped, other ideas will become more real than they are now.

We will not now go into a discussion on alchemy, but remember that what ancient alchemists had in view was that their concepts should not remain mere ideas but should lead to something. Whether they were justified is not the point for now (this may become the subject of another lecture). When they burned incense while holding their concept in mind or giving it voice, they tried to give it enough force to make the incense smoke assume form. They sought ideas that have the power to affect external realities of nature, ideas that do not remain merely within the egoistic part of human beings but can intervene in natural realities.

Why did ancient alchemists do this? They still had the idea that whatever occurred at the Mystery of Golgotha intervened in the course of nature; it was just as real and factual to them as a fact of nature. You see, this is the basis of a very significant difference that began in the second half of the Middle Ages, toward our own fifth age, which followed the Greco–Roman epoch. At the time of the crusades, during the twelfth to fifteenth and even the sixteenth centuries, there were some special natures—mainly women— who devoted themselves deeply to mysticism, to the degree that they experienced the inner results as a spiritual marriage, whether with Christ or another. Many ascetic nuns celebrated mystical marriages. I will not go into the nature of those inner mystical unions today, but something happened within them that could later be expressed only in words. In a sense, it subsisted in the ideas and feelings and in the words that clothed them.

In contrast to this, Valentine Andrea, as the result of certain concepts and spiritual connections, wrote his *Chymical Marriage of Christian Rosenkreutz*. This *chymical* (or, as we would say today, "chemical") marriage is also a human experience. However, when you go into the matter you find that this does not apply only to a soul experience but also to something not expressed merely in words but also grips the whole individual. It is not merely put into the world as a soul experience, since it was a real occurrence, or event of nature, in which a man accomplishes something like a natural process. In *The Chymical Marriage of Christian Rosenkreutz*, Valentine Andrea tried to express something more permeated with reality than merely the mystical marriage of Mechthild of Magdeburg, who was a mystic.

The mystical marriage of the nuns accomplished something only for the subjective nature of the human being; through the chymical marriage, a person would give oneself to the world. Through this, something was accomplished for the whole world, just as something is accomplished for the whole world through the processes of nature. This again is meant to be taken in a truly Christian sense. Those who thought more real thoughts also longed for concepts through which to understand reality better, even if only in the one-sided way of the old alchemists, concepts through which they could better grasp reality—ideas, in fact, that were actually connected with reality. Today, the age of materialism has veiled such concepts; and those today who believe they think correctly about reality are living in greater illusion than those despised individuals during the time of the ancient alchemists who strove for concepts that should help them to master it.

What can people today accomplish through their concepts? In our age in particular we have some experience of what they can attain through these empty illusions. Today the husks of ideas are worshipped idols; they have nothing to do with reality. We reach reality only by plunging down into it, not by forming any sort of idea at will; yet the difference between unreal concepts and those permeated with reality can be perceived in the ordinary things of the day, though most people do not recognize this. People are completely satisfied with the mere shadow of ideas that have no reality.

Suppose, for instance, someone today gets up and makes a speech in which one may say that a new age must come and is already manifesting—a completely new age in which all human beings will be measured only according to their own worth, valued according to what they can do. People today would admit that such words are in complete accord with the times. However, my dear friends, as long as ideas are mere husks, no matter how beautiful, they are not permeated by reality. It is not the point whether a man who is convinced that his own nephew happens to be the best man for the job should acknowledge the principle that all people should be put in the places to which their powers are best adapted. It is not the ideas and concepts one may have that are important; what is needed is to penetrate reality with those ideas and recognize it.

It is nice to have ideals and fine principles, and often even nicer to express them. But what we really need is to plunge into reality, recognize it, and penetrate it. We are plunging more and more deeply into what has brought about these sad times by continuing to worship the idols of the husks and shadows of ideas, by not learning to see that "such beautiful ideas and concepts" have not the slightest value, and by talking about them without the will to get right down to the realities and recognize them. If we do this, we shall not only find the substance, but also the spirit therein. It is the worship of idols, the mere shadows and husks of ideas, that leads us away from the spirit. It is the great misfortune of our time that people are intoxicated with fine words. It is also unchristian; the true basic principle of Christianity is that the Christ did not pour his teaching into Jesus of Nazareth, but poured himself in, which means that he united himself with earthly reality, was drawn into the reality of the Earth, so that he became the living message from the cosmos.

The New Testament, my dear friends, if read correctly, is the most wonderful means of education about reality. The New Testament, however, must gradually be rendered into our own language. The current translations do not give the complete original meaning. But once the old meaning is put into the direct language of our day, the Gospels will be the very best means of bringing "that power of thinking that is permeated with reality" to people. Nowhere can thought forms be found in them that lead to the husks and shadows of ideas. We need only grasp these things today in their deeper reality.

It may sound trivial almost to speak of the "intoxication of ideas," but this is so prevalent today that the ideas and concepts themselves, however beautiful they sound, are no longer the actual point. The important thing is that those who voice them should stand on reality. People find this difficult to understand today. Everything that emerges into the open today is judged by its content, and in fact by what is understood about that content. If this were not true, such documents—for instance, as the so-called Peace Program of President Wilson, which is entirely void of ideas, a husk, a mere conglomeration of the shadows of ideas—would never be taken as based on reality. Anyone having the power of discerning the reflections of ideas would know that this combination could at most work only by means of a certain absurdity, which might become a sort of reality. What is really needed is for people to try to find ideas and concepts truly permeated with reality; this, however, presupposes that the seekers themselves should be profoundly imbued with reality and be selfless enough to connect themselves with what lives and moves in reality. Much today is well-calculated to lead people entirely away from the search for reality, but such things go unobserved.

Yes, outer reality hangs together entirely with what people are continually developing. If they develop concepts void of reality, reality itself becomes confused and then follows conditions such as we have today. It is no longer possible to judge things by what we encounter externally today; we must form our opinions by studying what has been developing in human minds for years, decades, and even longer. That is what must be investigated. The whole thing depends on our not accepting the Christ from only his teaching, but that we should look at the Mystery of Golgotha in its actuality, or its reality; we should see that it was a fact that something SUPRAEARTHLY united with the Earth in the person of Jesus of Nazareth. We will then come to realize that morality is not merely something that fades and dies away when the Earth and even the fabric of the heavens become a grave; but even though present Earth and the present heavens become a grave, yet, just as today's plants will become mere dust while in the present plant, there is the seed of the next one; likewise, there is the seed of the next world in our world, and humankind is connected with this seed. However, this seed requires the connection with Christ so that it does not fall into the grave with the Earth, as a plant seed that has not been fructified falls into dust with the plant.

The most real thought possible is that the present moral order of the world is the germinal force for the future natural order. Morality is not merely a constructed thought; when permeated with reality, it exists in the present as a seed for future outer realities. A concept of the world such as that of Kant-Laplace, however—about which Hermann Grimm says that a piece of carrion that attracts a hungry dog is more appetizing—does not belong to that level of thought. A mechanical plan of the world can never penetrate to the thought that morality contains a force that is the seed of the natural, the nature of the future. Why can it not do this? Because it must live in illusion.

Just imagine, my dear friends, if the Mystery of Golgotha had not taken place, all would have been as the Kant-Laplace theory says. If you think away the Mystery of Golgotha from Earth, that theory would be correct. The Earth had to reach a condition so that, left to itself, it must inevitably lead the human race into the desolation of the grave. Things had to take place as they have, so that human beings might attain freedom through their relation to the Earth. They will not sink into the grave, because at the critical moment the Earth was fructified by Christ, because Christ descended, and because in Christ lies the opposing force to what leads to the grave—that is, the seed force whereby humankind can be born up once more into the spiritual world. This means that, when Earth becomes a grave, once it fulfils its destiny according to the Kant-Laplace theory, the seed concealed within it must not be allowed to fall into decay, but must be carried on into the future. Thus, the Christian moral plan of the world presupposes what Goethe calls "the higher nature in nature."

We might say that those who are able to think in the right way about the Mystery of Golgotha as a reality can also think thoughts and form concepts permeated by reality. This is necessary and what people must learn before anything else. In this fifth post-Atlantean age, people have either wanted to form concepts that intoxicate them or those that blind them. Intoxicating concepts are formed mainly in the areas of religion; those that blind are formed mainly in the domain of natural science. A concept like that of Kant (which, while admitting the purely natural ordering, placing the two worlds of knowledge and faith side by side, has yet only the moral in view) must lead to intoxication. Concepts based on moral grounds are able to intoxicate, preventing people from seeing that in this way they simply succumb to the stillness of the grave, into which all the world's moral plans have fallen and perished.

Or, again, such concepts as those of today's natural science, national economics, and (forgive the expression, which may be rather hard to swallow) even current politics may create blindness; they are not formed in connection with a spiritual concept of the world, but from the shreds of what people call actual reality (that is, in the physical sense). Thus, people see only as far as the end of their own nose, and blindly form opinions based on what they can see with their eyes and comprehend with mechanically acquired ideas between birth and death—without having formed any concepts permeated with reality by being imbued with the spiritual or having grasped spiritual reality.

Those who know see many sad things happening. For instance, it is absolutely appalling to someone who is not guided by mere words but by realities that it is possible today for people to be impressed simply by an assemblage of words, by a number of speeches that have indeed been printed. A highly honored person of our day has delivered speeches, and in his very first speech he immediately assumes the attitude that human beings in one aspect of their nature are completely related to the natural order, and that theologians are not acting correctly when they do not leave the order of nature to the scientists who investigate it. Those speeches go on to say that in regard to the natural order, the human being is simply a piece of machinery; however, the functions of the soul depend on this machinery; nearly everything then specified as functions belong to the soul. All these are then to be left to the investigators of nature. They leave nothing to comfort theology but the thought that all this has now been left to natural science, and all we have to do is to make speeches, to talk. After that, of course one can live only on the husks of words. Moreover, those speeches are composed so that they lack continuity. (I will return to this subject in coming lectures and go into it more fully.)

If you look closely into the thought that is supposed to be connected with the one immediately preceding it, you will find that it cannot possibly be thought of as connected. However, the whole thing sounds very good. In the preface to certain lectures "On the Molding of Life," it is stated that lately they have been attended by thousands of people, and that certainly many thousands more feel the need to comfort their souls at this serious time by perusing them. The lectures were given by the celebrated theologian Hunzinger, and I believe are in the Quelle & Meyer series "Knowledge and Education."[1] They are among the most dangerous literature of the day, because, though they sound enchanting, one's thinking simply becomes confused; the thoughts are disconnected and, if one strips away the fascinating words, nothing but nonsense. Yet these lectures were highly praised, and no one noticed the confused thoughts in them or stopped to test them; everyone was charmed by the shadow words.

It is continually necessary to point out what our age so desperately needs. Even history itself in our time is frequently no more than a mere shadow of ideas. How often what Fichte said to the German people is proclaimed abroad today. What he really said, however, cannot be understood unless one studies his whole life, a life so profoundly rooted in reality. This is why in my book *The Riddle of Man*[2] I tried to represent the personality of Fichte as he later became, showing how closely he was connected with reality from his childhood onward. I would indeed be glad if such words (as to the need for our thoughts and concepts to be permeated with reality) were not merely heard superficially but grasped profoundly—taken in and truly absorbed. Only then will a free and open vision, a psychic vision, be acquired for what our age needs so much. Every one of us should have this open soul vision. If we do not each make it a duty to consider the facts touched on here, we are not paying enough attention to the traffic today going on in the shadows and husks of words, nor to the fact that everything tends to lead people either into intoxicating concepts or to what blinds them.

---

1   A. W. (August Wilhelm) Hunzinger (1871–1920), Protestant theologian. His books include *Das Wunder: Eine dogmatisch-apologetische Studie* (The Wonder: A Dogmatic Anthropological Study; Leipzig: Quelle & Meyer, 1912); and *Hauptfragen der Lebensgestaltung* (Main questions of the Life Organization; Leipzig: Quelle & Meyer, 1916).

2   First published in 1916, *The Riddle of Man: From the Thinking, Observations and Contemplations of a Series of German and Austrian Personalities.*

I hope you will not take what has been said today as some sort of propaganda, but view it as an expression of actual facts. People certainly must and should live within their time, and when something is described they should not see it as everything that can be said on the subject. People should learn to strike a balance. It is quite natural that the world today should be confronted with impulses leading entirely to materialism. This cannot be prevented and is connected with the deep needs of the age. But a balance must be established.

One very prominent means of driving human beings into materialism is the cinematograph.[3] It has not been observed from this perspective, but there is no better school for materialism than the cinema. What we see there is not reality as people see it. Only an age that knows so little of reality as ours does, one that worships reality in a material sense as an idol, could believe that the cinema represents reality. Any other age would ask whether people actually walk along the street as seen at the cinema; people would ask themselves whether what they saw at such a performance really corresponds to reality.

Ask yourselves frankly and honorably: What is really most like what you see in the street? A picture painted by an artist, an immobile picture, or the dreadful, sparkling pictures of the cinematograph. If you ask yourselves quite honorably, you will admit that what the artist reproduces in a state of rest is much more like what you see. Hence, while people are sitting at the cinema, what they see there does not make its way into the ordinary faculty of perception; it enters a deeper, more material stratum than we usually employ for our perception. Etherically, people stare wide-eyed at the cinema; they develop eyes like those of a seal, though much larger—that is, etherically larger. This works in a materializing way, not only on what people have in their consciousness, but on their deepest subconsciousness.

---

3   A film camera that also serves as a projector and developer. It was invented in the 1890s by Léon Bouly (1872–1932).

Do not think I am abusing the cinematograph. I would like to say once more that it is quite natural it should exist, and it will attain far greater perfection as time goes on. This will be the road leading to materialism. But a balance must be established, and that can be created only as follows. With the search for reality being developed in the cinema, with this descent below sensory perception, people must also develop an ascent above it, an ascent into spiritual reality. Then the cinema will not harm people, and they can see it as often as they like. However, unless the balance is present, people will be led by such things not to a proper relationship to the Earth, but to becoming more and more closely connected to it, until finally they are entirely closed off from the spiritual world.

THE HUMAN SOUL AND THE UNIVERSE, PART 2

Berlin, March 6, 1917

I have told you about the three meetings that the soul must experience in the life between birth and death and that, even while still in that life, bring it into connection with the spiritual worlds. Today let us return to this subject, which on the last occasion was touched on in a preparatory way, as an episode, as it were. We will now go into it in more detail.

We noted that human beings in the midst of the intermediary state between sleeping and waking typically encounter the world related to our spirit self. I say "typically," because I am alluding to normal sleep at night. They then encounter the world in which we place the beings of the hierarchy we designate as that of angels. Thus, every time we pass through sleep, in a sense we pass through the world where those beings dwell, the world upward closest to our own physical world. Through this meeting we refresh and strengthen our whole spiritual being. Because of this, because in sleep we are connected with the spiritual world, no merely materialistic explanation of sleep, such as is put forward by conventional science, can ever satisfy.

Much of what occurs in human beings can be explained by the changes that take place in the body between waking up and going to sleep; we may try to explain sleep itself by means of these changes, but any such explanation will always be unsatisfactory because in sleep this meeting takes place and one comes into relation with the spiritual world.

This makes the whole difference. Thus, just when we consider the state of sleep, we can see that people, unless they consciously seek a relation to the spiritual world, arrive at only half-true concepts and ideas. These, in fact, because they become life, falsify it and eventually bring about great catastrophe. Indeed, these partially true concepts are even worse in some ways than those that are completely false, because those who form the partially true concepts and ideas rely on them; they are able to prove them because, being partly true, they can be proven. An attempt to disprove them would not bring further illumination, for these ideas are, after all, partially true. Such concepts actually falsify life even more than the entirely false ones do, because we can immediately recognize them as false.

One of these half-true concepts that today's natural science is giving up to some extent (though it is still widely believed) is an idea I have often alluded to: that we sleep because we are tired. We may say that this concept is only half true and is the result of a half-true observation. People think that the day's life tires out the body, and that we must sleep because we are tired. In previous lectures, I have often called attention to the fact that this concept does not explain why people of independent means, those who do no work at all, often fall asleep while the most invigorating matters related to the outer world are being discussed. It cannot be proved that such people have tired out and thus need sleep. This is absolutely incorrect. If we believe that fatigue compels us to sleep, we are only half observing. We notice that this is so only when we compare the observations made on the one side with what can be observed on the other when we come in contact with the other half of the truth. You will quickly see what I mean.

Sleeping and waking in individual human lives follow each other in rhythmic succession, yet people are free beings and can thus interfere with this rhythm. This is done more because of circumstances than what may be called freewill; nonetheless,

74

circumstances are the bases of free life. Another rhythm that we have often placed in the same order as sleeping and waking is that of the yearly seasons. Summer and winter alternate (leaving aside the intermediate seasons), but ordinary consciousness does not connect them correctly. It would not occur to anyone to say that, because the Earth is hard at work during the summer, unfolding the forces leading to the growth of plants and to much else, that it thereby grows tired and needs the rest of winter. Everyone would consider such an idea absurd and say that the onset of winter has nothing at all to do with the Earth's summer work, but that it is caused by the changing position of the Sun in relation to the Earth. Here, everything is supposed to be caused externally. In sleeping and waking, it all comes from internal fatigue.

One is just as incorrect as the other—or, rather, one is only partly true, and so is the other. The rhythm of sleeping and waking is exactly the same kind of rhythm as that of winter and summer. There is just as little truth in saying that we sleep only because we are tired as saying that winter sets in because the Earth has exhausted herself in summer. Both statements rest on the independent activity of a rhythm brought about by certain circumstances.

The rhythm between sleeping and waking comes about because the human soul needs the continually recurring meeting with the spiritual world. If we were to say we want to sleep and consequently feel tired; if we were to say that we enter the state in which we need one part of the rhythm, that of sleep, and consequently feel tired, we would be speaking more correctly than if we say we must sleep because we are tired. This whole question will become even clearer if we simply ask: What does the soul do when it sleeps?

Today's non-spiritual science lacks the requisite understanding and cannot reply properly to such a question. You see, while we are awake, we enjoy the outer world, and our enjoyment of this lasts our whole life through. We do not merely enjoy the outer world when we convey good food to our palate (which is the sense in which we generally speak of "enjoyment," because here it is directly applicable), but the whole time we are awake we enjoy the outer world; all life is enjoyment. Though there is much unpleasantness in the world and much that seems unenjoyable, this is only an illusion (which we will discuss in subsequent lectures in other connections). In our waking state, we enjoy the external world; in sleep, we enjoy ourselves. When we are in the body with our souls, we enjoy the outer world through the body. Likewise, when we are with our souls outside our body. In the life between birth and death, we remain connected with the body; even while outside it, we then enjoy our body. The condition of sleep, normal sleep, essentially means we are having a deeper experience of our body so that we enjoy it. We enjoy our body from outside. The correct interpretation of dreams—ordinary chaotic dreams—is that they reflect the enjoyment of the body that people experience in dreamless sleep.

You see, this explanation of sleep is approximately that of the need to sleep experienced by people of independent means, which I have already mentioned. We cannot easily believe that such individuals are actually tired; but we can very readily believe that they may be so fond of the body that they would rather enjoy that than what they often encounter from the external world. They actually love it so much and are so fond of enjoying it, that they may even prefer that to, let us say, listening to a lecture, which they may be too ashamed not to attend. Or perhaps a better example would be to say they would rather enjoy their body than listen to a difficult piece of classical music that sends them immediately to sleep when compelled to listen to it. Sleep is self-enjoyment.

Because in sleep, in normal sleep, we have the meeting with the spiritual world, our sleep does not therefore consist merely of self-enjoyment; it is also self-understanding, to a certain degree—self-understanding, or assessing oneself. In this sense, our spiritual training is really needed so that people may come to realize that in normal sleep they actually plunge down into the spirit and emerge from it when they wake up; it is necessary that they come to feel reverence for this meeting with the spirit.

Now, so that we do not completely fail to understand, I will return to the so-called enigma of fatigue; ordinary consciousness is very likely to lay hold of this point. It may say: Well, we really do feel tired, and when we are tired we feel sleepy. This point demands we make a truly clear distinction. Certainly we do get tired from the day's work, and while we sleep we are able to recover from our fatigue. This part of the matter is true; we can drive away fatigue by going to sleep. Nonetheless, sleep is not a result of the fatigue, but consists of the enjoyment we feel in ourselves. In this self-enjoyment, we acquire the forces through which we can drive away fatigue, but it does not follow that all sleep can do so. Whereas it is true that all sleep is enjoyment of self, it is not true that all sleep drives away fatigue. Those who sleep unnecessarily, those who sleep at every opportunity with no need for it, might as well bring about sleep in which there is no fatigue to be driven away, in which there is nothing but self-enjoyment. In this kind of sleep, people will certainly strive the whole time to drive away fatigue, because they are used to doing so while asleep. However, if there is no fatigue, as in the case of those well-to-do persons who fall asleep at a concert, they simply continue sweeping out the body, as they would do if the fatigue were present. When there is no fatigue, they go on sweeping out unnecessarily, with the consequence that they set up all kinds of bad conditions in the body. This is why such well-to-do people who sleep so much are the most troubled with all those fine conditions known as neurasthenia and the like.

Through a connection with spiritual knowledge, one may conceive a condition in which people will be conscious of living in a state of rhythm, in which one is alternately in the physical world and in the spiritual world. In the physical world one encounters external physical nature; in the spiritual world one meets with the beings who inhabit that world. We will be able to understand this matter fully by entering somewhat more deeply the whole nature of the human being from a particular point of view.

You know that it is customary to consider the outer science known as biology as a unity, divided necessarily into the head, breast, and lower part with the members attached to it. In ancient times, when human beings still possessed an atavistic knowledge, they connected other ideas with this division of the human being. The great Greek philosopher Plato attributes wisdom to the head, courage to the breast, and the lower emotions of human nature to the lower part of the body. What relates to the breast portion of the human being can be ennobled when wisdom is added to courage, becoming wise courage, or wise activity. And what is considered the lower part of human beings, that belonging to the lower parts of the body, Plato says it is "clothed with the Sun" when it is thoroughly radiated by wisdom.

Thus, we see how the soul is divided and attributed to the different parts of the body. Today, those of us who have spiritual science (which was not similarly attainable for Plato) speak of these things in much greater detail. In speaking of the fourfold division of the human being, we begin at the top by speaking of one's "I." All that we can call our own in the sense of soul and spirit during our physical life between birth and death works through the instrument of the physical body. Concerning each of the four principles of the human being, we can ask, with which part of the human body is each physically connected? A real and sufficiently penetrating spiritual observation shows us that what we call the human "I," strange as it may seem (for the truth is often very different from what the superficial consciousness supposes), between birth and death the human "I" is connected physically with what we call the lower part of the body.

The "I," as I have often said, is really a baby as compared to the other parts of human nature. The seed of the physical body was already laid down in the ancient Saturn period, the seed of the ether body during ancient Sun, and the seed of the astral body during ancient Moon. However, the "I" was only

78

laid down in our own Earth period; it is the youngest member of the human being. It will attain the stage at which our physical body now exists only in the far-distant period of Vulcan. The "I" is attached to the lowest bodily part of the human being, and this part is really always asleep. It is not organized so that it can bring to consciousness what takes place within it; what takes place there, even in the normal waking periods, is ceaselessly asleep. We are no more conscious of our "I" as such in its reality, in its true being, than we are of our processes of digestion. The "I" of which we are conscious is merely a reflexive concept, the image of which is reflected into our head. We never really see or realize our "I," whether in sleep, when in normal conditions we are quite without consciousness, or in our waking state. The "I" is then also asleep. The true "I" does not itself enter our consciousness; nothing but the concept of "I" is reflected there. On the other hand, between sleeping and waking, the "I" really comes to itself; but those in normal deep sleep know nothing of it, being themselves still unconscious in deep sleep during the Earth period. Thus the "I" is in fact connected with the lowest human bodily part. During the day, in the waking time, it is connected with the body from within, and during sleep from without.

As far as the body is concerned, however, what we call the ether body is connected with the head. Through the peculiar organization of the head, the ether body is able to be constantly awake when in the human body when connected with the physical head. We may therefore say that the "I" is connected with the lowest parts of our body, and the astral body with our breast part. The heart (in terms of activities of which we are not fully conscious but have only a dream-like awareness) beats and pulses under the influence of the astral body. When the head thinks, it does so under the influence of the ether body. We can thus further differentiate our physical body because, in its entirety, it is connected with the whole outer world.

If we now move on to the second principle in human nature, what we call the astral body, we find that regarding the

COSMIC AND HUMAN METAMORPHOSES

instrument through which it works, from a certain point of view it is connected with the breast part of the human being. Of all that goes on in this astral body working through the breast part, we can, in fact, only dream. As earthly human beings, we can know something of the "I" only while asleep; consciously we know nothing. Of all that the astral body works in us, we can only dream. This is really why we dream constantly of our feelings, or the sentiments living within us. They actually live a sort of dream life within us. The human "I" is actually outside the region that we human beings, with our ordinary sensory consciousness, can comprehend, because it is continuously asleep. The astral body is also in a sense outside that region, too; it can only dream. With respect to both of these we are, whether asleep or awake, in reality in the spiritual world; we are really and truly within that world.

Now we see a remarkable connection. The "I" is connected with the lowest parts of the body; the astral body with the heart; the ether body with the head; and the physical body with the whole outer world, or the environment. During the waking condition, the whole physical body is really in constant connection with the outer environment. Just as we are in relation to the outer environment with our whole body, likewise our ether body is in relation to our head, the astral body to the heart, and so on. This will show you how truly mysterious the connections are in which we live in the world. In reality, things are generally just the opposite to what the superficial consciousness may lightly assume.

The lowest parts of human nature are at present the least perfected forms of the human being; hence, these parts of the body, as such, correspond to what we have called the baby—our "I." Innumerable secrets of human life are concealed in what I am discussing here, countless secrets. If you go into this subject thoroughly, you will understand above all that the whole human being is formed from spirit, but at different stages. The human head is formed from spirit, but is more fully molded, belonging to a later stage of formation than the breast, of which indeed one might say that it is just as much a metamorphosis of the head as, in the sense of Goethe's theory of the metamorphoses of plants, the leaf is a metamorphosis of the flower. If we consider the rhythm between sleeping and waking from this point of view, we may say that during the waking hours the "I" actually dwells in all the activities in the human body, in all the lowest activities, which finally culminate in the formation of our blood. The "I" is present in all these activities during the waking hours. These activities are those that are, in a sense, at the lowest stage of spirituality. Of course, everything connected with the body is spiritual. Now it must be noted carefully that during the waking hours the "I" exists at the lowest stage of spirituality, but during the hours of sleep it exists at the highest stage with respect to the human being.

Consider this: when we look at the head that we as human beings have today, that head is, in its outer form, the strongest manifestation of the spirit. It best represents spirit, its greatest manifestation. Here the spirit has entered matter most deeply. Consequently, here less is left behind in the spirit itself. Human beings have spent so much work on the head, to make its outer form a manifestation of the spiritual, that little is left behind in the spirit. The lower members of the human bodily nature in terms of their outer formation are the least spiritualized and have been least worked upon in a spiritual sense. Because of this, more of what pertains to them is left behind in the spiritual. The head, as head, corresponds least to the spiritual, because it has more spirit within it; the lower part of the body corresponds most, because it has the least spirit within it. However, during the hours of sleep the "I" dwells in this greater portion of spirit that does not dwell within the bodily nature.

Just reflect on this wonderful equalizing process. In terms of the body, human beings possess a lower nature into which the "I" immerses itself during the waking hours, but this lower nature is "lower" only because the spirit has worked less upon it, because it retained more of the spirit in the spiritual region. Yet, during sleep the "I" dwells in what it thus held back. During sleep, the "I" is even now already present in what human beings will not develop until a later epoch, which only then they will be able to develop and unfold. Presently, this is merely indicated and as yet little developed in human bodily nature. Hence, when the "I" becomes aware of the conditions in which it finds itself during sleep, when it really becomes conscious of this, it will be able to say to itself: while asleep, I am within my holiest human predisposition; when I emerge from sleep, I pass from this holiest part of me into what gives only a faint indication of it.

Through spiritual science, such matters must find their way into our feelings and inner sentiments and live there. A magical breath of holiness will then spiritualize life itself. We will then have a definite and positive idea of what is called the Grace of the Spirit, or the Holy Ghost. We will connect the realization of this collective existence that runs its course in the rhythm between sleeping and waking with the idea that we are allowed to take part in the spiritual world, one is allowed to dwell in it. Once we have realized and felt this idea, or concept, one is allowed within the spiritual world; one is thus given grace. One is permeated with the spiritual world, which is inaccessible to ordinary earthly consciousness. When we have thoroughly filled ourselves with that thought, we will have learned also to look up to the spirit that reveals itself just as clearly, I might say, between the lines of life, as the outer world of nature reveals itself to our external eyes and ears.

The age of materialism, however, has led people far from awareness of the Grace of the Spirit being radiated into and permeating their whole collective existence. It is immensely important that we regain this consciousness; the depths of our souls are more affected by the general materialism prevalent today than we suppose. Yet the human soul is now generally too weak to realize in itself the concepts that could lift it out of and above materialism. One such concept is that of the holiness of sleep, which once understood, we would then ascribe all those thoughts and concepts in our waking life that do not connect us with matter, to the inward activity of spirit that follows sleep. We would not then view our waking state, which unites us with matter, as the only important thing to us. This would be like considering the winter the important time for the Earth; we should rather contemplate the whole. In terms of the Earth, we contemplate it as a whole when we connect winter with summer; in terms of the human beings, we contemplate them as a whole when we consider the day (the human being in relation to matter) in connection with sleep (our relationship to the spirit).

A superficial observation might lead one to say that, in their waking state, people are bound up with matter and cannot know anything of the spirit—but that they nevertheless do know something of the spirit, even while awake. Human beings have memory, and this memory works not only in one's consciousness, but also subconsciously. If we had no memory, sleep would be of no use to us at all. I want you to fix this fact very firmly in your minds, because it is very important. No matter how much we sleep, if we did not have memory sleep would not help us. If we had no memory, we would be forced to believe that there is nothing but material existence. It is only because we preserve the memory of what we experience during sleep in our subconscious—though we may know nothing of it in our ordinary consciousness—only because we have a subconscious memory of what we then go through that we have not surrendered entirely to a materialistic mode of thinking. If people do not think only materialistic thoughts, if they have any sort of spiritual ideas during the day, it is because their memory is active. Human beings, as we are now, as earthly beings, come into contact with the spirit only during sleep.

The point is that, if we were nonetheless now able to develop a strong consciousness like that during sleep—as people of ancient times did under certain circumstances—we would never consider doubting the existence of spirit. We would be able to recall not just subconsciously but also in full consciousness what we encounter during sleep. If people were to experience in full consciousness what they go through in sleep, it would be absurd to deny the existence of spirit, just as it would be for people to deny the existence of tables and chairs while awake. The crucial point is that humankind should again gain the ability to properly appreciate the meeting with spirit in sleep. This can be done only by making the images of one's daily experiences sufficiently vivid; it can be done only by delving deeply into spiritual science.

In this study we occupy ourselves strongly with ideas drawn from the spiritual world. We compel our head (the ether body of our head) to picture things that are connected in no way with outer phenomena, but have reality only in the world of the spirit. This requires the application of more effort than picturing things that are real in the world of matter. Indeed, this is the real reason so many people do not become involved in spiritual science. People find all sorts of reasons against it, saying that it is illogical. If such people were forced to prove in what way it is illogical, they would be embarrassed, because it can never be proved that spiritual science is illogical. The real reason for turning away from spiritual science arises from something very different.

In a scientific refutation, we may be allowed to be a bit impolite; thus, we may say that one's nonrecognition of spiritual science arises solely from laziness of soul. No matter how industrious certain educated people may be in regard to all the concepts of outer phenomena, when it comes to the force needed to understand matters of spirit, they are idle and lazy. It is because they will not arouse the necessary force in themselves that they refuse to recognize spiritual science. It requires more effort to think the ideas of spiritual science than it does to think ordinary thoughts related to sensory phenomena, which really come on their own. However, ideas unrelated to material things must be *thought.* We must wrestle with them and make a great effort. It is this shrinking from the necessary effort that is behind the nonacceptance of spiritual science, and this is what we must recognize.

When real effort is exerted to accept concepts and ideas not connected with matter and to think them through, activity is aroused in the soul that can gradually develop awareness of what takes place between falling asleep and waking, with the realization that a meeting with the spirit takes place then. People will certainly need to unlearn certain ideas. Just consider how little some spiritual leaders are capable of developing such ideas.

What I am about to relate now occurs less frequently these days, but during their youth many current leaders were frequently so deeply immersed in the life of their day that they drank themselves into the state called *Bettschwere* in German. They drank so much that they established the necessary gravitation. Well, in such cases, people's ideas, as well as their feelings about what happens during sleep, are certainly not suited to elucidate the whole significance of sleep. People may be extremely educated about everything related to matter, but they cannot then naturally gain an understanding of what happens to them between falling asleep and awaking.

When people make the necessary effort to think completely through ideas unrelated to material things, they will be able to develop an understanding of what I have called the "first meeting," the meeting with the spirit during sleep. The world will fall into a state of decadence unless such understanding illumines life soon and fills it with sunlight. If people do not take up these ideas, what will be the basis of their concepts? They will be able to form concepts only by observing external conditions, by studying the outer world. Ideas formed only in this way leave the inner human being, the soul part, in a state of inertia. The portion of the human being that must be strongly exercised in spiritual concepts and ideas under other circumstances is rendered inert and unused; it dies.

And what is the result? It is that one becomes blind, spiritually blind in relation to the world. If one develops no ideas or concepts except those formed under the influence of outer impressions, a person becomes spiritually blind, and spiritual blindness does indeed prevail greatly in this materialistic age. In science, this is injurious only up to a point, but in practical life such blindness to the real world is extremely harmful. You see, the further we descend into matter, the more things correct themselves in this materialistic age. When people build a bridge, circumstances force them to learn the proper rules of construction; otherwise, the bridge may collapse when the first vehicle crosses it.

It is easier to apply incorrect concepts when trying to cure someone, because the cause of death or wellness can never be proved. This does not mean that the ideas put into practice are necessarily the right ones. If we wish to work in the realm of the spirit, it is a far more serious matter; it is, therefore, especially serious that matters generally known as the practical sciences—politics, national economics, and the like—are in a bad way. In this materialistic age, people have gotten used to being guided by impressions and ideas formed in the outer world and applying these to doctrines of national or political economics, and in this way their ideas have become blind. Almost all that has been developed thus far along these lines are only blind ideas. It therefore follows as a natural consequence that people with these blind notions are strung along by events, yielding blindly to the course of those events. If they then intervene in events in this condition...well, what can we expect?

Such blind ideas are one possibility that forms as a result of not taking up spiritual science. Another is that, instead of being stimulated to form ideas by outer circumstances, people may allow themselves to be stimulated from within—that is, they allow, in a sense, only what lives in the emotions and passions to arise in the soul. In this way, people do not acquire blind ideas, but what we might call intoxicated ideas. People today who are acknowledged materialists constantly swing back and forth between blind ideas and intoxicated ideas. Blind ideas are those in which people allow themselves to be blinded to what is going on, so that when they intervene they do so in the clumsiest way possible. Intoxicated ideas are those in which people give way only to their emotions and passions, confronting the world in such a way that they do not really understand things, but only love or hate everything. Thus, everything is judged according to love or hate, sympathy or antipathy.

We gain clear-sighted ideas and concepts only when we exert effort in our soul to acquire spiritual ideas, on the one hand, and on the other develop our feelings for the great concerns of the world. When we lift ourselves to the thoughts about the great connections as given to us through spiritual science, which brings only laughter from the materialistic worldview—ideas about the ages of Saturn, Sun, and Moon and about our connection with the Universe—when we fructify our moral feelings with the great goals of humanity, we can then rise above all those emotions displayed as sympathy and antipathy toward everything in the surrounding world. These emotions cannot be overcome in any other way.

Without a doubt, it is necessary to purify much that lives today through spiritual science. After all, people do not allow themselves to be cut off entirely from the spiritual world. People do not actually allow themselves to be cut off at all, but only seem to. I already pointed out the way this seems to be done. On the one hand, when people assert as true only the physical and their impressions of the outer world, forces intended for the spirit nevertheless remain within them. However, they then direct those forces to a false area and give themselves up to all sorts of illusions. This is why it is primarily the most practical and materialistic people who are subject to the strongest illusions and give in to them.

We see people going through life denying the existence of spirit and laughing heartily when told of anyone having spiritual experiences. "He sees ghosts!" they exclaim. And having said this, they imagine they have ended the matter. They themselves certainly do not see ghosts in their sense of the word. But they merely believe they see no ghosts; in fact, they see ghosts incessantly; they see them all the time. We can test a person who is thus rooted in a materialistic view of the world, and it will become clear that in regard to what the next day may present, such a person gives in to the worst illusions. Such surrender to illusions is simply a substitute for the spiritual, which the person denies. When people deny the spiritual, they must necessarily give in to illusion. It has been said that it is difficult to prove the illusions that exist in the various areas of life, but they are prevalent everywhere—actually everywhere. People are truly fond of giving in to illusion. Consider this frequent experience, for instance. A person may say, "If I invest my money in a certain undertaking, it may be used for brewing beer. I refuse to use my money in that way. I will not be a part of that." So the money is deposited in a bank. The bank, without the person's knowledge, invests the money in a brewery. It makes absolutely no difference objectively, but this individual is under the illusion that the money is not being used for base purposes such as beer.

Naturally, it may be argued that this is far-fetched, but it is not; it really is something that rules all life. People today do not bother becoming truly acquainted with life and learning to see through it, but this is very important. It is immensely important that we come to know what surrounds us. This is not easy today, because life has become so complicated. Nevertheless, what I have drawn attention to is true.

You know that under certain circumstances one might easily imagine an absurd situation. For example, there was once an arsonist (this is a true story) who ran from a house that he had set on fire, having planned things to allow himself time to do so. He was caught and brought before the authorities. When questioned, he answered that he thought he had done a good deed and that he was blameless; rather it was the workers, who had left a lighted candle in the house when they left it in the evening. If the candle had burned out at night, it would have set the house on fire. Therefore, he set the fire himself before dark. In either case the house would have been on fire. He set it on fire so that the fire would be extinguished sooner, since a house may be saved if it is burning in the daytime, whereas at night it is a more complicated matter, and the whole house would have burned to the ground.

When asked why he did not put the candle out, he replied, "I am a teacher of humanity. If I had blown out the candle, the workers, who were the ones to blame in the matter, would have continued to be careless, but now they can see for themselves what happens when they forget to blow out their lights."

We may laugh at such an example as this, because we are unaware that we are continually doing the same. People constantly act just as the man who did not put out the lighted candle but set fire to the house. But we do not notice this when we are disturbed by our emotions and passions, which intoxicates ideas, and when the whole thing relates to the spiritual world. If we accustom the soul to the elasticity and flexibility needed to form spiritual ideas, we will mold our thought truly to find its way into life and properly adapt to it. If we do not do this, our thought will never be fit to deal with life; it will not even be affected by it, except superficially. This is why (turning now to the deeper side of the matter) the materialistic age really leads people away from any connection with the spiritual world. Just as we undermine our physical health if we do not get proper sleep, likewise we undermine our soul life if we do not spend our waking hours in the right way. If we give way only to outer impressions and live without awareness of our connection to the spiritual world, we are not awake in the right way. Just as people might undermine their physical health because of tossing and turning and restless sleep, people also undermine their spiritual health by yielding to impressions of the outer world and being subject only to physical matter. This prevents experiencing that first meeting with the spiritual world in the right way, as I have said. In this way, people lose any possibility of connecting themselves properly with the spiritual world during their physical existence. Such people are thereby cut off from the connection with the world in which we spend our time when not incarnated and into which we ourselves pass when we go through the gates of death.

Human beings must again come to understand that we are not here just to build in the physical universe during our physical existence; we must come to understand that, during the whole of our existence, we are connected with the whole world. Those who have already passed through the gates of death want to work with us on the physical world. Their cooperation appears to be only a physical activity with us, but everything physical is an outer expression of the spirit. The age of materialism has estranged people from the world of the dead. Spiritual science must reestablish the friendship between them. The time must come again when we no longer block the work of the dead for the spiritualization of the physical world by estranging ourselves from them.

The dead cannot participate with hands in physical events; they cannot accomplish physical work in such a direct way. It would be foolish to believe this. The dead can work in a spiritual way, but to do so they must have the instruments placed at their disposal; they need the spiritual matter that lives here in the physical world. We are not only human beings; we are also instruments—instruments for spirits who have passed through the gates of death. As long as we are incarnated in physical bodies, we use a pen or a hammer or an axe; when we are no longer incarnated in physical bodies, the instruments we use are human souls themselves. This is based on the peculiar way that the dead perceive, which I will just touch upon again. (I mentioned this subject here once before.)

Suppose you have a small vessel containing salt. You can see it; the salt appears as a white substance or white powder. The fact that you see the salt as a white powder relies on your eyes. Your spirit cannot see the salt as a white powder, but if you put a little salt on your tongue and taste the peculiarly salty taste, then it is possible for the spirit to become aware of it. Every spirit can perceive the taste of the salt in you. Every spirit, including the human souls that have passed through the gates of death, can perceive all that takes place in human beings through the outer world. Within us, the world of senses extends to our tasting, smelling, seeing, and hearing; likewise, the world of the dead reach down into what we hear, see, taste, and so on. The dead share in our experiences of the physical world, because those experiences belong not only to our world, but also to theirs. They belong to their world when we spiritualize our experiences in the outer world with spiritual ideas. Unless we do this—if we experience merely the laws of matter—to the dead this is something they cannot comprehend, and it remains dark.

To the dead, a soul devoid of spirit seems dark. Consequently, the dead have become estranged from earthly life in our age of materialism. This estrangement must be eliminated. An inner common life between the so-called dead and the so-called living must take place. But this can come about only when people develop forces in their souls that are truly spiritual—that is, when people develop ideas, concepts, and images that deal with spiritual matters. When people make an effort to reach the spirit in their thinking, they gradually reach it in reality. It indicates that a bridge now crosses between the physical and the spiritual worlds. This alone can lead human beings across from the age of materialism to the time when they face realities, neither blindfolded nor intoxicated, but with vision and poise. Having learned to see through the spirit, they will attain vision and poise, and through the feelings and sentiments aroused in them by the great concerns of the world, people will gain the right balance between sympathy and antipathy in relation to what our immediate surroundings demand of us.

We shall continue the considerations of these subjects in our next lecture, and go more deeply from this aspect—the ideas to be gained from the spiritual world.

HUMANKIND AND THE SUPRAEARTHLY

Berlin, March 13, 1917

Today, let us again dwell a while on the considerations referred to as the "three meetings." We have said that the two alternating states of sleeping and waking in which we live in the short course of twenty-four hours are not merely what they appear to ordinary physical life. We said, rather, that during every one of these twofold periods, we have a meeting with the spiritual world. We explained this by saying that the "I" and the astral body, which separate from the physical and etheric bodies during sleep—being breathed out as it were when going to sleep and breathed in again on waking—that during the hours of sleep the "I" and the astral body meet with the world we think of as belonging to the hierarchy of the angels. Our own human soul will also belong to that world when it has formed the spirit self. In this, what we are accustomed to calling in religious life the Holy Spirit rules as highest directing principle. In some detail, we have gone into this meeting we have with the Holy Spirit in the spiritual world during each of our normal periods of sleep. We need to understand very clearly that, with the development of humankind during Earth evolution, changes have taken place in regard to these matters.

So, what actually takes place while people are asleep? Well, I think I made this clear in the previous lecture, from the standpoint of what happens within the human being. Considered in terms of our relationship to the universe, in a sense human beings imitate the rhythm in the world order that is established in any part of the Earth, since half of the twenty-four hour period is day and the other half night. Of course, it is always day somewhere on Earth, but a person lives in only one part of it. Because this rule is a given fact, wherever we live, we imitate the rhythm between day and night in our own rhythm of sleeping and waking. The fact that this rhythm is broken in modern life—that people are no longer compelled to be awake during the day and asleep at night—is connected with human progress in evolution, in the course of which human beings have raised themselves above the objective course of the world. People now have only the one rhythm of day and night within them and no longer the two rhythms working together. In a certain sense, these rhythms work for the universe, or macrocosm, at one time, and at another time for human beings, or the microcosm. However, they are no longer in unison. Human beings have in this way become, in a sense, independent from the macrocosm.

Now, in ancient times when, as we know, there was a certain atavistic clairvoyance in human beings, with respect to this rhythm they were more in harmony with the great course of the world order. In ancient times, people slept at night and were awake during day. Consequently, the whole circle of human experience was different from what it is now. However, human beings have, in a sense, had to be lifted out of this parallel with the macrocosm, and being thus torn away we have been compelled to stimulate an inner independent life of our own.

We cannot say that the main point is that because people slept at night that they did not observe the stars; they did observe them, notwithstanding the fables of conventional science about worship of the stars. The essential thing is that human beings were then organized differently into the whole world order. While the Sun was positioned on the other side of the Earth and, consequently, did not exercise its direct activity on the part of the Earth on which certain people lived, they were able in their "I" and astral body (which were outside their physical and etheric bodies) to

94

devote themselves to the stars. They thus observed not only the physical stars, but also perceived the spiritual aspect of the physical stars. They did not actually see the physical stars with their outer eyes, but saw the spiritual part of the physical stars. Hence, we must not view what is related of the ancient star worship as though the ancients looked up to the stars and then made up all sorts of beautiful symbols and images.

According to modern science, it is very easy to say that, in ancient times, the imagination was very active—that people imagined gods behind Saturn, Sun, and Moon, that they pictured animal forms in the signs of the zodiac. However, it is only the imagination of learned scientists that works this way, inventing such ideas. It is true, however, that in the state of consciousness of the ancients' "I" and astral body, this did seem to them as we have described—that they really saw and perceived those things. In this way, human beings had direct vision of the spirit that is the soul of the universe; they lived with it. In reality, we are suited for the Earth only in regard to our physical and ether bodies; the "I" and astral body in their present condition are suited to the spirit that is the soul of the universe, as described. We may say that they belong to that area of the universe; but humankind must develop far enough to experience the innermost being of the human "I" and astral body and to have experiences within them. For this purpose, the external experience that was present in ancient times had to disappear, or become blurred, for a time.

The consciousness of communication with the stars had to recede; it had to be dimmed, so that people's inner being could become powerful enough to enable them, at a certain time in the future, to learn to strengthen it enough to find the spirit as spirit. Just as the ancients, when asleep, were united every night with the spirit of the stellar world, likewise human beings once connected with that spirit also during the course of each year. But, as time went on, in the course of the year human beings came into contact with a higher spirit of the starry world and, in a sense, with the events of that world. While sleeping at night, the forms of the stars in their calm repose worked upon human beings. Through the course of the year, they were affected by the changes connected with the Sun's course of the year; they were connected, so to speak, through the Sun's course with the Earth's destiny for the year, caused by her passage through the seasons and especially through summer and winter.

You see, although some traditions still exist that relate to those ancient human experiences when asleep at night, only a few remain of those even more distant times (or rather few traced back to their origin) when humankind took part in the secrets of the year's course. The echoes of these experiences still persist, but they are little understood. If you search among the myths of the various peoples, you will constantly encounter what proves humankind then knew something about a conflict between winter and summer, summer and winter. Again, conventional erudition sees only the symbolic creative imagination of the ancients; it says that we in our advanced times have progressed past that. These were, however, real human experiences, and they played a significant and profound role in the whole spiritual civilization of the ancient past. There were mysteries that taught knowledge of the secrets of the year. Just consider the significance of such mysteries. These were different in very ancient times from what they became later—during the history of ancient Egypt, ancient Greece, and to some extent even the earlier Romans. We will, therefore, consider the mysteries that passed away with the older civilizations of Egypt, Greece, and Rome.

There was still awareness of the connection between the Earth and the whole universe in those mysteries. At the time, it was customary for suitable persons to be subjected to a certain psychic process, but this would no longer work today. They could, during a certain number of days in winter, be sent to specific locations to be as it were "receiver stations" for the universe, or supraearthly universe, and to receive what it could communicate to the Earth at such times, as long as the times provided a sufficiently receptive receiver.

Today's Christmastime was then not exactly the most important time, but approximately so, though the exact time is not
important for the moment. Let us suppose the time was between
December 24 and early January. Through the special position of
the Sun to the Earth, this season is one in which the universe con-
veys something to Earth that it does not at other times. During
this season, the universe speaks more intimately to the Earth
than at other times. This is because the Sun does not develop its
summer force at this time; the summer force has withdrawn in a
certain respect. The leaders of the ancient mysteries took advan-
tage of this time to make it possible in certain places—organized
with the help of specially prepared persons—to receive the inner
secrets of the universe, which came down to Earth during this
intimate duologue. We may compare this today with something
much more trivial, though the two can be compared.

We know that "wireless telegraph communication" is based
on the fact that electric waves are set in motion and are further transmitted without wires, and that in certain places an
instrument called a coherer [radio detector] is installed. Through
its peculiar arrangement, this makes it possible for the electric
waves to be received and the coherer activated. The whole thing
depends entirely on the arrangement and formation of the metal
filings in the coherer, which are shaken back into place once
the waves have passed through it. Now, if we assume that the
secrets of the universe, or supraearthly universe, pass through
the Earth at the special time mentioned, it would be necessary to
have an instrument to receive them, because those electric waves
would pass by the receiving station with no purpose unless the
right instrument is present and attuned to receive them. Such an
instrument is needed to receive what comes from the universe.

The ancient Greeks used their Pythian oracle, or priestesses,
for this; they were trained for and especially sensitive to what
came from the universe, and they were able to communicate its
secrets. Those secrets were later taught by those who perhaps
had long been unable themselves to act as receivers. Nonetheless,

the secrets of the universe were disseminated. This took place, of course, under the sign of the holy mysteries, a sign about which the present age, which no longer has any feeling for the holy, has no concept. In our age, clearly the first matter would be to "interview" the priests of the mysteries.

Now, what was the greatest requirement of those priests? In a certain sense, they had to know that, if they became acquainted with what streamed from the universe for the fructification of earthly life, and especially if they used it in their social knowledge, having thus become much smarter, they must be able to establish the principal laws and other rules for governing during the coming year.

At one time, it would have been impossible to establish laws or social rules without first seeking guidance from those who could receive the secrets of the macrocosm. Later ages have retained dim and dubious echoes of this greatness as superstitious fantasies. On New Year's Eve, when people pour melted lead into water to learn the future of the coming year, this is only the superstitious remnant of that great matter I have described. In this way, they tried to fructify the human spirit so that they could carry into earthly existence what could spring only from the universe; the desire was that people should live on Earth in such a way that their lives would not consist only of what can be experienced here, but also what can be drawn from the universe. Likewise, it was understood that during earthly summertime we are in a very different relation to the universe, and that during summer the Earth cannot receive any intimate communications from the universe. The summer mysteries were based on such knowledge; they were intended for a very different purpose, which I need not go into today.

Now, as I have said, even less concerning the secrets of the year's course has come down to us in tradition than about matters related to the rhythm between day and night and between sleeping and waking. In those ancient times, however, when human beings still had a high degree of atavistic clairvoyance, through which in the course of the year they could experience the intimate relations between the universe and the Earth, they were still aware that what they thus experienced came from that meeting with the spiritual world, which people today cannot have every time they sleep. It came from the meeting with the spiritual world, in which dwell the spiritual beings we think of as part of the world of the archangels—where human beings will one day live with their innermost being after developing life spirit during the Venus period. This is the world in which we must think of Christ, the Son, as the directing and guiding principle. Humankind experienced this meeting in all ages, of course, but it was previously perceived through atavistic clairvoyance. We, therefore, call this meeting the "meeting with the Son." Through the course of the year, people anywhere in the world experience this when they make Christmas in their winter. Thus, during a year, people actually go through a rhythm that imitates the seasons of the year, in which people meet and unite with the world of the Son. We know that, through the Mystery of Golgotha, the being we call the Christ has united himself with the Earth's course. At the very time this union took place, direct vision into the spiritual world became blurred, as I just explained.

We see this objective fact: the Event of Golgotha is connected directly with the alteration in human evolution on Earth. Yet we may say that there were times in the Earth's development when, in the sense of the old atavistic clairvoyance, human beings came into relation with Christ through awareness of the intimate dialogue between the Earth and the macrocosm. A belief held by certain modern educated individuals, students of religion, is somewhat justifiably based on this. This is the belief that an original, primal revelation was once given to the Earth. It came about as described. It was an old, primeval revelation. All the various religions on Earth are fragments of that original revelation, fragments that have fallen into decadence.

What is the position, then, of those who accepted the Mystery of Golgotha? They can express an intense inner recognition of the spiritual substance of the universe, saying that, in ancient times, what could be perceived only through the duologue between the Earth with the cosmos has now descended. It lived in a human being; it appeared in the man Jesus of Nazareth during the Mystery of Golgotha. Recognizing the Christ who lived in Jesus of Nazareth, recognizing the being formerly perceptible only to atavistic human clairvoyance during certain seasons of the year must be emphasized increasingly as a necessity for the spiritual development of humanity. The two elements of Christianity will be then united as they actually should and must be if Christianity on the one hand and humanity on the other are to develop in the right way.

The fact that the legend of Jesus Christ in the old Christian traditions was part of the annual celebrations of Christmas, Easter, and White Sunday is connected with this. Moreover, as I stated in a previous lecture, the fact that the Christmas festival is kept at a fixed date while Easter is regulated according to the heavenly constellations is also connected with this. Christmas is celebrated in accordance with earthly conditions; it is always held in the very depth of winter, and this hangs together with the meeting with Christ, the Son, the meeting that actually takes place in that season. Christ, however, is a being of the macrocosm. He descended from there, yet is united with it. This is expressed by aligning Easter with the heavens in spring, according to the constellations of Sun and Moon. The Easter Festival is intended to show that Christ belongs to the whole universe, just as Christmas should point to the descent of Christ to Earth. Thus it was proper that what belongs to the seasons of the year through their rhythm in human life should be inserted into the course of the year as is done. This is so profound in connection with the inner human being that it is actually correct that the festivals relating to the Mystery of Golgotha should continue to be in harmony with the rhythm of the great universe, and not be subject to the alteration that has happened in modern cities to the hours of sleeping and waking.

Now, among the things perhaps most faulted in spiritual science by certain religious sects is that the Christ impulse, according to spiritual science, must be connected once again with the whole universe. I have often stated emphatically that spiritual science takes nothing away from religious traditions with respect to the mystery of Jesus Christ; rather, to them it adds the connection surrounding the mystery extending, as it does, from the Earth to the whole universe. Spiritual science does not look for Christ only on Earth, but also in the entire universe.

Here we have something in which human beings should not yet exercise their freewill, something in which each year consciousness should come to them, so that, although people can no longer contact the great universe through atavistic clairvoyance, there is still something living within them that belongs to the universe and expresses itself in the course of the year.

Indeed, it is difficult to understand why certain religions so strongly condemn this connection of the Christ impulse with cosmic events. One could understand such an attitude if spiritual science were trying to do away with the Christian traditions; but since it only adds to them, this should not be a reason for censure. Thus it is, however, and the reason is that people do not wish anything to be added to certain traditions.

There is nonetheless something very serious behind all this, something very important to our age. I have often pointed out the fact (also mentioned in the first of my mystery plays[1]) that we are approaching a time when we can speak of a spiritual return of Christ. I need not go more fully into this today; it is well known to all our friends. This Christ Event will, however, not merely be an event satisfying the transcendental curiosity of man, but it will above all bring to their minds a demand for a new understanding of the Christ impulse.

Certain basic terms of the Christian faith that should surge through the whole world as holy impulses—at any rate, through

---

1   See Rudolf Steiner, "The Portal of Initiation," in *Four Mystery Dramas*.

the world of those who wish to take up the Christ impulse—are not understood deeply enough. I will now call to your memory just the significant and incisive words "My kingdom is not of this world" [John 18:36]. These words take on new meaning when Christ appears in a world that is truly not of this world— the world of the senses. It must be a profound attribute of the Christian worldview to cultivate an understanding of other human views and concepts, the sole exception being rough and crude materialism. Once we understand that all earthly religions are the remnants of ancient vision, then only will it be a question of taking what was perceived in this way seriously enough. Later on, because humankind was no longer organized for such vision, the results of that former vision filtered through only in fragmentary form into the various religious creeds. This can be recognized once again through Christianity.

Through Christianity a profound understanding can be gained, not only of the great religions but also of every form of religion on the Earth. It is easy enough to say this, but at the same time very difficult to cause the adoption of such views by people. Nonetheless, they must become part of people's convictions throughout the world. Christianity, insofar as it has spread over the Earth until now, is only one religion among many, one creed among a number of others. This is not the purpose for which it was established; it was founded to spread understanding over the whole Earth. Christ did not suffer death for a limited number of people, nor was he born for only a few, but for all. In a certain sense, there is a contradiction between the necessity that Christianity should be for everyone and the fact that it has become one of many creeds. It is not intended to be a separate creed, and it can be that only because it is not understood in its full and deep meaning. Cosmic understanding is needed to grasp this deep meaning.

Today, one must struggle for words with which to express certain truths that are so far removed from humanity now that we lack words to express them. One must often express the great truths through analogues. You will recall that I have often said that Christ may be called the Sun Spirit. From what I have said today about the yearly course of the Sun, you will see that there is some justification for calling him the Sun Spirit. However, we cannot form an idea of this or picture it unless we keep the cosmic relation of Christ in view, unless we consider the Mystery of Golgotha as a real Christ mystery, something that definitely occurred on this Earth, yet has significance for the whole universe and happened for the whole universe.

Today, people are in conflict with one another about many things on Earth and are at variance on many questions. People are at odds in their religious beliefs and think that they have differences regarding their nationality and many other matters. Such lack of unity brings about times such as those in which we now live. People are not of one mind, even with regard to the Mystery of Golgotha. No Chinese person or Indian will immediately accept what a European missionary says about the Mystery of Golgotha. To those who see things as they are, this fact is not without significance. There is, however, one thing about which people are still of one mind.

It hardly seems credible, but it is a common truth and one we have to acknowledge—that when we reflect on how people live together on the Earth, we have to wonder that there may be anything left about which they are not at odds. Yet there are still matters about which people agree. One such example is people's view regarding the Sun. The Japanese, Chinese, and even the English and Americans do not believe that one Sun rises and sets for them and another for the Germans. They still believe that the Sun is the common property of all; indeed people still believe that anything extraterrestrial is the common property of all. They do not even dispute that or go to war over such matters. And that can be taken as a sort of analogy.

As mentioned, these things can be expressed only by comparisons. When people once realize the connection of Christ with these things that people do not dispute, they will not dispute about him but will learn to see him in the Kingdom that is not of this world but belongs to him. However, until human beings recognize the cosmic significance of Christ, they will not agree on matters over which unity should prevail. We will then be able to speak of Christ to Jews, Chinese, Japanese, and Indians, just as we speak to Christian Europeans. This will open up an immensely significant perspective for the further development of Christianity on the Earth, as well as for the development of humankind on the Earth. Ways must be found to arouse sentiments in human souls that everyone will be able to understand equally.

This is one thing that will be demanded of us in the time that brings the return, the spiritual return, of the Christ. A deeper understanding will come about in that time, especially with respect to the words "My Kingdom is not of this world"— a deeper understanding that there is something in the human being that pertains not only to the Earth, but also something supraearthly that lives in the annual course of the Sun. We must come to feel that just as the soul rules the body in the individual human life, likewise something spiritual lives in everything that goes on outside, in the rising and setting stars and in the bright sunlight and fading twilight. And just as we belong to the air with our lungs, we also belong to the spiritual part of the universe with our souls. We do not belong to the abstract spiritual life of an outgrown pantheism, but to the concrete spirituality that lives in each individual being.

Thus we will find that there is something spiritual that belongs to the human soul—which is the human soul itself. And we will find that this has an inner connection with what lives in the course of the year, just as a person's breath does, and that the course of the year with its secrets belongs to the Christ being, who went through the Mystery of Golgotha. We must soar high enough to connect historical events on the Earth in the Mystery of Golgotha with the great secrets of the world, or macrocosmic secrets. Something extremely important will arise from such an understanding—knowledge of human social needs. A great deal of social science is practiced today, and all sorts of social ideals are debated. Certainly nothing can be said against this, but all these things will have to be fructified by what will spring up in humankind through realizing the course of the year as a spiritual impulse. Only by vividly experiencing the image of the Mystery of Golgotha each year, parallel with the course of the year, can we become inspired with real social knowledge and feeling.

What I am saying here certainly must seem very odd to people of the present day, yet it is true. When the year's course is again generally felt by humanity as in inner connection with the Mystery of Golgotha, then, by attuning the feelings of the soul with both the course of the year and the secret of the Mystery of Golgotha, a true social ruling will be the true solution, or at any rate the true continuation of what is today so foolishly called (in reference to what is actually in view) "the social question." People will have to acquire, precisely through spiritual science, knowledge of the connections between humankind and the cosmos. This will surly lead them to see more in this universe than do the materialists of today.

It is the very things to which people attribute the least importance that are really the most important. Today's materialistic biology, or natural science, compares humankind with animals, though it certainly admits a certain difference in degree. In its own domain, such science is of course correct. But what it leaves out of account completely is the relationship of humankind to the directions of the cosmos. The animal spine (and here the exceptions prove the rule) runs parallel with the surface of the Earth; it is directed out into the universe. The human spine is directed toward the Earth. For this reason, human beings are quite different from animals, above and below. The "above and below" in human beings determine our whole being. In animals, the spine is directed toward the infinite distances of the macrocosm; in human beings, the upper part of the head, the brain, and humans themselves, are inserted into the whole macrocosm. This is of enormous significance. This brings about something that establishes a relationship between the spiritual and physical in human beings, and through this our spiritual and bodily parts become subject to the conditions of above and below.

I will have more to say about this, but today I will just allude to it in a sort of outline. This "above and below" characterizes what we may consider "going out of the 'I' and astral body during sleep." Human beings, with their physical and ether bodies, are really inserted into and form part of the Earth while awake. During the night time, with our "I" and astral body, we are inserted, in a certain sense, into what is above.

Now we may ask: Well, how is it, then, for other opposites in the macrocosm? There is also an opposite that, in human beings, can be described as "front and back." In respect to these, too, human beings are inserted in a different way into the whole universe than animals or, indeed, plants are. Human beings are inserted so that we correspond both in front and behind to the course of the Sun. This "front and behind" is the direction that corresponds to the rhythm in which we participate in living and dying. Just as human beings express, in a sense, a living relation between "above and below" in sleeping and waking, likewise in our living and dying we express the relation between "front and behind."

This "before and behind" corresponds with the course of the Sun; so that for human beings, "front" means toward the east, and "behind" toward the west. East and west form the second direction of space, the direction we really mean when we say that the human soul forsakes the human body not in sleep, but at death. When the soul leaves the body, it goes toward the east. This may still be found only in those traditions in which, when people die it is said that they "entered the eternal east." Such old traditional sayings will one day (as they are even now) be viewed by the educated as merely symbolic. Some such platitudes as this will be stated: The sun rises in the east and is a beautiful sight; therefore, when one wanted to speak of eternity, the ancients spoke of the east. Yet this corresponded to a reality, and indeed one more closely connected with the annual course of the Sun than with the course of the day.

The third difference is between inner and outer, above and [inner
below, east and west, inner and outer. We live an inner life, and ↓
we live an outer life. The day after tomorrow [March 15, 1917] outer
I will give a public lecture on this inner and outer life, entitled
"The human soul and the human body." We live an inner and an
outer life. These form opposites in human beings just as great
as above and below, east and west. Whereas in the course of
the year human beings have more to do with what I would call
a representative delineation of the whole course of life, we may
say, too, that when we speak of an inner and outer life in connection with human life and death, we refer to the whole course
of a human life, especially insofar as it has an ascending and a
descending development.

We know that, up to a certain age, we go through ascending development. Our collective growth then ceases; it remains
at a standstill for a while, and then retrogrades. Now it hangs
together with the collective course of one's life, so that in its
early stages one's whole body is then more connected in a natural, elemental way with the spiritual. I might say that at the
beginning of life, we are constituted in the very opposite way
from what we are in midlife when we attain the zenith of our
ascending development. In the first part of life, we grow, thrive,
and increase; afterward, our descending development begins.
This is connected with the fact that one's physical forces are
then no longer in themselves forces of growth, because the
forces of decay are intermingled with the forces of growth.
The inner nature of human beings is then connected in a similar way with the universe, as at our birth, at the beginning of
life, our outer bodily nature is connected with the universe.
A complete turning round takes place. This is why in midlife
people today go through the meeting with the Father Principle
(the spiritual being we think of as part of the hierarchy of the
archai) in an unconscious condition. We then meet with that
spiritual world in which we will dwell once we have completely
developed his spirit body.

Now, we might ask: Is this, too, in some way connected with the whole universe? Is there anything in the life of the universe connected in a way similar to the meeting in midlife with the Father Principle, just as the meeting with the Spirit is connected with the rhythm of day and night, and the meeting with the Son with the rhythm of the year? This question may be asked. Well, now, my dear friends, we must keep in mind and hold firmly to the fact that, in terms of the meeting with the Father Principle, as well as that with the Spirit Principle, we are lifted *above* rhythm, which does not run quite parallel with the human being. People are not all born at the same time but at different times; therefore, the course of human lives cannot be parallel; but they can inwardly reflect some spiritual cosmic event.

Do they do this? Well, you see, if we recall what is stated in the booklet "The Education of the Child in the Light of Spiritual Science"[2] and in other books and lecture courses, we know that during our first seven years we especially build up our physical body; in the next seven years, our ether body; in the following seven years, our astral body. Then for seven years, we form the sentient soul; from twenty-eight to thirty-five, we form the intellectual or reasoning soul; and during this period we have the meeting with the Father Principle. This takes place during that time—not that it extends over the whole period, but occurs during those years—so that we may say people prepare it in their twenty-eighth, twenty-ninth, and thirtieth years. In most cases, this meeting takes place in the deepest subconscious regions of the human soul.

Now, we must assume that this corresponds to some event in the universe—that is, we must find something in the universe that represents a course, or rhythm. Just as the rhythm of day and night is twenty-four hours, and the course of the year 365 days, we should be able to find something similar in the universe, which would have to be more comprehensive. All of this is connected with the Sun, or at least with the solar system. Just as the

---

2   Originally an article published in the journal *Lucifer-Gnosis* in 1907. See *The Education of the Child and Early Lectures on Education.*

twenty-eighth, twenty-ninth, and thirtieth years are more comprehensive than a period of twenty-four hours, and just as the
365 days are more comprehensive than any other period, likewise
something even greater must be connected with the Sun, something corresponding with this third meeting.

The ancients correctly considered Saturn as the most distant
planet from our solar system; it is the farthest out. From the
standpoint of physical astronomy, it was justifiable to add Uranus
and Neptune to our system; but they have a different origin and
do not belong to the solar system. Therefore, we may speak of
Saturn as the outermost planet of our system. Now consider this.
If Saturn traces the boundary of the solar system, we may say
that in its circuit round the Sun it travels around the outermost
boundaries of the solar system. When Saturn travels around this
and returns to its starting point, he describes the extreme limits
of the solar system. When Saturn has traveled around the Sun
and returned to his starting point, he occupies the same relation
to the Sun as he did to begin with.

Now, Saturn (according to the Copernican cosmic system)
takes twenty-nine to thirty years to complete his course, which
lasts therefore about that duration. Here then, in the circuit of
Saturn around the Sun, which is not yet understood today (the
facts are really very different, but the Copernican cosmic system
has not yet advanced enough to understand them), in the course
of Saturn we find a connection, which extends to the farthest
limits of the solar system, with the human lifespan. Thus, this is
an image of the Saturnian circuit, insofar as the human lifespan
leads to the meeting with the Father.

This also leads us out into the macrocosm. Thus, my dear
friends, I think I have shown you that our innermost being cannot be understood unless considered in connection to the extraearthly. The extraearthly, being spiritual, is organized into
something that in a sense turns it toward us visibly. But what
it manifests visibly is also merely an expression of the spiritual. Lifting people above materialism will not take place until

knowledge has progressed enough to lift itself above the mere comprehension of earthly connections and ascend again to grasp the world of the stars and the Sun.

I pointed out on a former occasion that many things about which today's scholastic wisdom does not allow itself to dream are connected with these matters. People today believe they will one day be able to generate living beings in laboratories from inorganic matter. Materialists make the most of this today, but one does not need to be a materialist to believe that a living being can be created in the laboratory from inorganic matter. The alchemists, who were certainly not materialists, testified that they could make *homunculi,* but today this is understood in a materialistic sense. The time will come, however, when it will be realized and felt inwardly when approaching someone at work in a laboratory, because living beings will indeed be produced in the laboratory from lifeless materials—we will feel compelled to say, "Welcome to the star of the hour." This cannot be brought about at any hour, but will rely on the constellations. Whether life arises from the lifeless will depend on extraearthly forces that come from the universe.

There is much that is connected with these secrets, and we will speak of these things again soon, because it is now possible to say something about these subjects. Speaking of this, Louis Claude de Saint-Martin, "The unknown philosopher," says in many places in his book *The Errors and the Truth*[3] that he thanks God they are shrouded in secrecy. They cannot remain secret, however, because humanity will need them to develop further. But one thing is necessary, my dear friends—that people should regain earnestness and feeling for the holiness of all these things, without which the world will not use such knowledge properly.

We will speak of these matters again in the next lecture.

---

3   *Des erreurs et de la vérité, Ou les hommes rappelés au principe universel de la science* (available in French in facsimile editions).

ERRORS AND THE TRUTH

Berlin, March 20, 1917

Today I would like to introduce a sort of historical survey into this series of lectures, not so much to make this a lecture on history as to draw attention to various matters concerning today's spiritual attitude that directly surrounds us.

In 1775, a very remarkable book appeared in Lyons, which as early as the year 1782 found its way into certain circles of German spiritual life. Its effects were much greater than is generally thought. Above all, the result was such that it had to be somewhat suppressed by the principal impulse of the nineteenth century. This book is extremely interesting, especially to those who, in the interests of spiritual science, wish to learn what happened from the earliest times down to our own. I allude to *Errors and the Truth* by Louis Claude de Saint-Martin [1743–1803].

Anyone who picks up this book today, whether in its original language or in the careful German edition by Matthias Claudius with its beautiful preface, will find it very difficult to understand. Claudius himself admits this, even at the end of the eighteenth century. In his fine preface he says, "Most people will not understand this book; I do not understand it myself. But what it contains has sunk so deeply into my heart that I think it must be allowed into the widest circles." The people who will be least able to understand this book are those whose knowledge is based on the physical, chemical, and similar concepts of the world as taught in today's schools or acquired as ordinary education, and who lack any real knowledge of these matters. Neither will people understand this book who base their present views of the times (we will not use the word *politics*) on what they glean from the ordinary newspapers or from what is reflected from those newspapers into magazines of the day.

Following the two public lectures I gave last week, there are several reasons why I would refer to this book today. In them I spoke on the nature and the principles of humankind and on the connection between the human soul and the human body, referring to the way we will one day speak of those connections once the knowledge available now through natural science that cannot be applied is viewed in the right way. Those who have a thorough knowledge of spiritual science must realize that once the knowledge of natural science is appreciated correctly it will no longer be possible to speak about the relationship between the life of imagination, or feeling, and the will to the human organism. It may be that a beginning has been made in these two lectures of what must come, though it may be postponed for a long time by the great resistance made in the external world—not by science, but by the scientists themselves. However long it may take, people must eventually consider the relation between the human soul and body as outlined in those two lectures.

In those lectures, I spoke of these matters because it is necessary to speak of them in 1917—that is, considering all the investigations of natural science and other human experiences. For example, one could not have spoken in that manner during the eighteenth century. Such matters would have been discussed in a very different way then. The great significance of the fact I have repeatedly mentioned is not sufficiently realized—that somewhere around the end of the first third of the nineteenth century, in the thirties or forties, a crisis of exceptional magnitude from a spiritual perspective occurred in the development of European humanity. I have often mentioned this, saying that the tide of materialism then reached its height.

I have also frequently pointed out the frivolous way our time is often called a "period of transition." Of course, every period is one of transition, and it is absolutely correct to say this of our own. The point, however, is not so much to claim that any particular time is a period of transition, but to establish the substance of that transition. Then we will certainly encounter certain turning points that represent deep incisive moments of transition in human development. One such transition occurred at the time mentioned, though it goes unnoticed today.

Thus, it is easy to see that today we must speak in a very different way about the mysteries that confront humankind. We must use very different expressions and study the subject from a different perspective than would have been the case in the eighteenth century. Perhaps no one in the eighteenth century spoke with the intensity of Saint-Martin, who called the attention of natural science at the time to problems not unlike those we are discussing here. In everything he said, Saint-Martin stood in the fading light of the old age, and not as we stand in the glimmering light of a new age. Unless we consider the perspective I am about to discuss, it might seem a matter of indifference whether one studied Saint-Martin at all, whether one absorbed or not the peculiar form of ideas aroused in him by Jakob Böhme. And this might indeed be a matter of indifference unless a very different, much more significant standpoint were in question, which I am about to discuss today.

Let us relate a concrete case. In trying to point out the possible errors of humankind owing to its life philosophy, as well as to point out the path to truth, Saint-Martin in his book *Errors and the Truth* uses, in the most practical and objective way, the ideas and concepts current in certain circles up to and into the eighteenth century. It can be seen by the way he writes that he was thoroughly accustomed to using them. For example, we find that, in trying to explain the relation of humankind to the whole cosmos and to ethics, Saint-Martin employs the three principal ideas that play such a great a role with Jakob Böhme and Paracelsus—mercury, sulfur, and salt, the three main concepts through which people tried then to understand the sensory world and human beings. These three elements were investigated in the search for a key to understanding outer nature and humankind. Modern humanity, in the sense of today's natural science (as one must speak), can no longer use those expressions in the same way.

Today, it is impossible to think as one did during the eighteenth century about mercury, sulfur, and salt. In speaking of these, a threefold nature was then in view, which people today could represent only according to natural science by dividing the human being as I have done, into a being of metabolism, rhythm, and nerve. These three compose the whole human being; every part of us belongs to these three. If we suppose that any one part does not belong to these three—perhaps the bones—the discrepancy would be only apparent, not real. People of the eighteenth century knew that the whole complexity of a human being could be understood by gaining a comprehensive grasp of mercury, sulfur, and salt. Today, of course, when ordinary people speak of salt, they are referring to the white substance they have on the dinner table, or if they are chemists, the salts with which one works in a laboratory. When speaking of sulfur, people generally think of matches, while chemists think of their many experiments for the transmutation of sulfur. As for mercury, one immediately thinks of quicksilver and such.

People of the eighteenth century did not think in this way. Indeed, today it is very difficult to imagine what lived in the souls of that time, when people spoke of mercury, sulfur, and salt. In his own way, Saint-Martin asked himself: How should I divide the human being if I take the body as the image of the soul? He decided that, first one must consider the human instruments, or organs, of thought. He puts this differently, but we must translate a little, since it would otherwise be too lengthy.

One must first study the human being with respect to the organ of the head. What is the main component of the head?

What comes into consideration there? What is the truly active agent in the head...or as we would say today, "in the nervous system"? Saint-Martin's response is "salt." He does not mean white table salt or the chemist's salt, but the totality of forces at work in the human head when a person forms ideas. He considers the whole outer nature and activity of salt as only manifestation, an external manifestation of the forces at work in the human head.

He then asks: What is the element that works mainly in the human breast? According to the division of the human being I presented in last Thursday's lecture, we would ask this: What works in the breathing human being? Saint-Martin's reply is "sulfur." Thus, according to him, everything connected with the functions of the chest is governed by actions that originate in sulfur or have the nature of sulfur. He then asks: What works in the rest of the human being...today, we would say, "in the human metabolism." His answer is that mercury is at work there.

Thus, in his own way, Saint-Martin composes the whole human being. In the way he sometimes throws things together disjointedly, we see that he stands in the fading evening twilight of that whole system of thought. Conversely, we see that, standing in the twilight this way, he could grasp an enormous number of grand truths that one could still understand then but have since been lost. He expressed matters by using the three concepts of mercury, sulfur, and salt. Thus, in the book *Errors and the Truth,* there is a very fine treatise (complete nonsense, of course, to modern physicists) on thunderstorms—on thunder and lightning. In it, he shows how one may use mercury, sulfur, and salt to explain bodily human nature, on the one hand, and on the other explain atmospheric disturbances. Sometimes, they worked together within human beings, at another time in the world outside. In human beings, they engender what may spring up as a thought or impulse of will, while outside in the world the same elements engender, for instance, lightning and thunder. As we have noted, what Saint-Martin expounds could well be understood in the eighteenth century; it belonged to the mode of thought of that time.

To present-day physicists, it would be complete nonsense. It is precisely in relation to thunder and lightning that there is a flaw in modern physics, which is obliged to be rather less disciplined with respect to these phenomena. It teaches that when clouds—one charged with positive, the other with negative electricity—are near each other and discharge their electricity, a thunderstorm results. Any bright young student would notice that before the teacher starts electrical experiments, any traces of dampness are carefully wiped from the instruments, for nothing can be done with electricity where dampness is present. A student may ask the teacher, "Aren't clouds damp? How can electricity, then, work in them, as you say?" The teacher probably replies, "You are a silly child; you don't understand." One would hardly be able to give any other answer today.

Saint-Martin tried to explain how through the salt in the air, mercury and sulfur may be connected in a special way, in a way similar to that in which saltpeter and sulfur are united in gunpowder through charcoal; likewise, through a particular transmutation of the elements of mercury and sulfur through salt, explosions can occur. This exposition on the laws of that time is very smart. I cannot now go into it more deeply, but let us consider the question more historically. Saint-Martin especially proves in a fine way that in certain properties of the clouds that lead to thunderstorms, one can verify the relationship of lightning to salt, or what he called salt. In short, in his own way he fights the materialism that was then beginning to dawn, for he had the basis of a traditional wisdom behind him, which found an industrious worker in him. In so doing he strove to find an explanation of the world in general, and after having made the mentioned explanations that use the elements, he goes on to an explanation of Earth's origin. In this, he is not so foolish as those born after him, who believe in a mist or nebula as the origin of all things, and who think they can find the beginning of the cosmos by means of physical concepts. He starts using his imagination immediately to explain the origin of the world. In the book *Errors and the Truth,* when he speaks on this subject we find a wonderful wealth of imaginative ideas, of true imaginations, which, like his physical ideas, can be understood only in connection with the age in which he lived. We could not use them today, but they show that beyond a given point he tried to grasp things by means of imaginative cognition.

Then, having tried this, he goes on to comprehension of the historical life of humankind. Here, he tries to establish how that can only be understood by allowing for the real spiritual impulses from the spiritual world that from time to time found their way into the physical plane. He then tries to apply all this to the deeper nature of man, by showing how the Bible story of the Fall in Paradise is, according to his imaginative cognition, based on definite facts, how human beings passed from their primal condition to the existing one. He then tries to understand the historical phenomena of his own time, as well as that of all the time of history, in the light of the Fall from spiritual life into matter. I am not upholding this, but it must be mentioned. Naturally I do not wish to put the doctrine of Saint-Martin in the place of spiritual science, our Anthroposophy. I am relating history only to show how far ahead of his times he was.

As we read *Errors and the Truth,* chapter after chapter, we encounter one notable remark. We see that he speaks from a rich fullness of knowledge and that what he offers is only the outer rind of the knowledge living in his soul. This is indicated in various passages in which he says something like this: If I were to go deeper into this, I would be giving out truths that I may not express. In one place, he even goes so far as to say, "If I were to say all that could be said on this subject, I would have to give out certain truths that, so far as most people are concerned, are better left veiled in the deepest darkness of night." True spiritual scientists can read much between the lines of these passages; they understand why these remarks appear in specific parts of certain chapters. There are some matters that cannot be discussed by means of assumptions. It will not be possible to speak of such things until the impulses of spiritual science have grown into moral, ethical impulses—when people have acquired certain elevated convictions through spiritual science that enable them to speak about certain matters in a way that is different from what may be done in an age when such strange scientific figures as Freud and those around him. But these things will become possible one day.

In the final third of his book, Saint-Martin goes on to certain political subjects. It is hardly possible today to do more than indicate how the kind of thinking he uses can be related to the way people "think" (as they call it) today. This is a forbidden subject. I can say only that his whole attitude throughout the last third of his book is very remarkable. If we read this chapter today, we must do so while keeping it clearly in mind that the book was published in 1775, and that the French Revolution took place later. This chapter must be considered in connection with the French Revolution; we must read much between the lines in this particular chapter. Saint-Martin proceeds as an esotericist, I might say. Anyone lacking the organ of perception for the profound impulses found in this chapter would probably be quite satisfied with its introduction, in which Saint-Martin says, "Let those connected with the ruling powers of the Earth or connected in any way with the government understand that I am not trying to get into good standing with them. I am a friend of all and everyone." After having excused himself in this way, he goes on to say things are mere child's play compared to Rousseau's remarks. But I cannot say any more about this.

In short, we must realize the deep incisive significance of this man, who had a school behind him, and without whom Herder, Goethe, Schiller, and the German Romanticists could not be imagined, as he himself cannot be thought of without Jakob Böhme. Nonetheless, when we read Saint-Martin today, allowing ourselves to be influenced by what he says, we feel, as I have just said, that there would not be the least purpose in putting what one has to say to the public in the form Saint-Martin uses. That would be of no use now as I try to give a picture of the world, as I did in the previous two public lectures and shall again in the next. On the one hand, based on spiritual science, it must be correct and, on the other, be fully justified according to the most minute discoveries of natural science today. The mode of formulating ideas that Saint-Martin uses is no longer suited to the way people must think today, nor to the way people they must (and rightly so) formulate their thoughts. While traveling, when we go from the region of one language to that of another, at that moment we can no longer speak the language of the first; similarly, it would be foolish today to use Saint-Martin's form of thinking. And it would be all the more foolish because, lying between us is that great dividing line in spiritual evolution that falls in 1842, around the first third of the nineteenth century.

You can see by this, my dear friends, that it is possible in the spiritual development of humanity for a certain kind of thinking to fade into the twilight. In studying Saint-Martin, however, we do not feel that his words have been exhausted. On the contrary, we feel that an enormous amount of undiscovered wisdom remains in his works, and that much could still be taken from it. Yet, on the other hand, it was necessary in the human spiritual development that his way of thinking should end and that another should begin. This had to be. In the former, the external world was just beginning; it had reached only its most external phases of materialism. Thus, we cannot correctly understand what really happened unless we survey longer periods of time and apply what spiritual science wishes to stimulate in us to greater epoch. Of course, what Saint-Martin presented at the end of the eighteenth century, then only in its dawn, subsequently took a different form.

At that time, something came to an end on Earth. Not only did the ideas ruling Jakob Böhme, Paracelsus, Saint-Martin, and others descend into the twilight in a relatively short time because it was not possible to carry them further; but a very curious change also took place in the mode of feeling. In Saint-Martin, we see this phenomenon of the human mind's twilight in regard to the study of nature. However, the same phenomenon can also be traced in another way if we focus on the almost parallel decline of theosophy—the dimming, diminishing theosophical philosophy of life.

True, Saint-Martin is generally called a theosophist, but in describing and discussing him, I think of a theosophy directed toward natural science, rather than the more religious form of theosophy then prevalent and called by that name. Theosophy in the particular form that then reached its climax ruled (I was going to say) in southern Germany, though it may be more accurate to say "in Swabia." Although it was already on the decline there, it had reached a certain maturity, and among its most prominent followers, the figures of Bengel and Oetinger[1] stand out, surrounded by many others. I will simply name those I know best: Friederick Daniel Schubart; Hahn the mathematician; Steinhofer; the schoolmaster Hartmann, who had a great influence on Jung-Stilling, and even a certain influence on Goethe and knew him personally; and Johann Jacob Moser.[2] A good number of remarkable minds in comparatively humble circumstances, who did not even form a connected circle, but who all lived when Oetinger's star shone in the firmament. Oetinger, born in 1702 and dying in 1782, lived through almost the whole eighteenth century; he was as Prelate in Murrhard. A very remarkable personality, in whom all that the whole circle contained was concentrated, in a sense.

---

1   Johann Albrecht Bengel (1687–1752), a Lutheran pietist clergyman and Greek-language scholar known for his edition of a Greek New Testament; Friedrich Christoph Oetinger (1702–1782) studied philosophy and theology at Tübingen and was impressed by the works of Jakob Böhme.

2   Christian Friedrich Daniel Schubart (1739–1791), a Swabian poet; Philipp Matthäus Hahn (1739–1790), a Swabian theologian, mathematician, mechanic, and astronomer; Friedrich Christoph Steinhofer (1706–1761), a philosopher and theologian; Israel Hartmann (1725–1806), teacher at an orphanage in Ludwigsburg; Jung-Stilling (Johann Heinrich Jung, 1740–1817), writer, optician, and professor; Johann Jacob Moser (1701–1785), professor of law and writer on law and theology.

It was an echo of this eighteenth-century theosophy that influenced Richard Rothe, a professor at the University of Heidelberg and other universities.[3] He wrote a fine preface to a book edited by Carl August Auberlen, *The Theosophy of Friedrich Christoph Oetinger.* In his preface, Rothe, who represents a traditional echo of that circle, reminds us, in his convinced acceptance of theosophy, of those great theosophists just mentioned. On the other hand, we can clearly see in the way he speaks of Oetinger in his preface, that he feels he is standing behind a period of twilight, even in regard to the secrets of life with which he was concerned as a theologian. The preface was written in 1847. I would like to quote some of it here so that you may see how, within Richard Rothe (who was then in Heidelberg), one lived who looked back in his thinking to Oetinger and saw in him a man who above all strove, in his own fashion, to decipher the Old and the New Testaments—who tried to read them with theosophical understanding of the world. Rothe looked back at that method of reading the scriptures and compared it with the way he had been taught to read them, which was then customary. He died in the sixties and was himself merely an echo. In this sense, Richard Rothe says something very remarkable:

> Among the men of this school, to which Bengel with his *Apokalyptica* belongs, Oetinger occupies a foremost place. Not satisfied with the theology of the schools of his time, he thirsted after a richer, fuller, and at the same time purer understanding of Christian truth. Orthodox theology did not satisfy him; it seemed shallow to him, and he wanted more than that—not that it asked too much of his faith, but that the deeper spirit within him wanted more than that. He did not object to the supernaturalism of the orthodox theology of his time, but considered rather that the latter did not take the supernatural seriously enough. His innermost soul rebelled against the spiritualism that reduced world realities

---

3   Richard Rothe (1799–1867), professor of Protestant theology and director of a clerical seminary. The book quoted is available in facsimile reprints.

of Christian faith to mere abstractions, to mere thought pictures. Hence his fiery zeal against all forms of idealism.

Such a saying might seem strange, but it has to be understood. By *idealism*, the German understands a system that lives only in ideas, whereas Oetinger, as well as Rothe, worked for true spiritual life. They were true spirits who pushed history forward, not like what Ranke and others with their pallid notions have described as so-called ideas of history.[4] As though it were possible for mere *ideas* (one really does not know what word to use in speaking reality) to wander through history and carry the whole thing further. The followers of Oetinger wished to replace the abstract and dead with the living. Hence, Oetinger's fiery zeal against any idealism; hence, too, his realism, which, in his energetic search for "substantial" concepts, actually did tend toward materialism, though this was not his intention. The concepts he was trying to find were those that could really grasp the spiritual and not merely talk about an ideal archetype behind phenomena, but real, solid (substantial) thoughts and ideas, such as those that look for the spirits behind created phenomena.

Rothe continues:

His leaning toward nature and natural science is intimately connected with this fundamental scientific tendency. The lack of appreciation and the tendencies of the idealists to despise the world of nature were foreign to him. He felt that behind crude matter there is a very real existence. He was profoundly permeated by the conviction that without the world of senses there could be no real, true existence, whether divine or creative. This is a startling and new legitimizing of historical authority, and we see not only in Oetinger but also in earlier contemporary theosophists and

---

4   Leopold von Ranke (1795–1886), a German historian considered a founder of modern source-based history. He set the standards for much of later historical writing, introducing such ideas as reliance on primary sources (Empiricism), emphasizing narrative history and especially international politics.

especially in the philosophical writings of Jakob Böhme, the original scientific tendency of the Reformation breaking through again, as shown in this thirst for a true understanding of the natural world.

The kind of realism, for which Oetinger longed, comes to "life in its innermost being in Christianity" (according to Richard Rothe); if transplanted into any other spiritual movement, it would become weaker, especially in regard to its own peculiar doctrine. It is capable of bearing a completely different, richer, Christian world of wonder than that of the idealism to which we have all been accustomed from childhood, which is governed by a fear of believing too strongly in the actuality of divine matters and the fear of taking the word of God too literally. Indeed, such Christian realism requires exactly the wonder world that is unfolded in the doctrine of the last things.[5] It cannot therefore, be led astray in its eschatological hopes by a compassionate shaking of the head by those who believe that only they are right. For Christian realism, it does not seem possible to arrive at a thoughtful understanding of created things and their history without clear and definite thinking about the final result of the world's development, which is the object and aim of Creation, for only thus can light and meaning come into human concepts. This Christian realism does not shrink from the thought of a real, bodily, and therefore truly living spirit world, nor from real contact with that world by humankind, even in its present state. The reader admits how true this all seems in the pages of Oetinger.

This refers to a time when human beings did not look for ideas of the natural world, but for a living world of spirit. Indeed, Oetinger tried to bring all the treasures of knowledge then available to humanity to his assistance in establishing a living connection with the spiritual world. What existed behind such a man?

---

5   Or *eschatology,* a branch of systematic theology that deals with the doctrines of the last things (*ta eschata*). The "four last things": Death, Judgment, Heaven, and Hell.

He was not like a person of our day, who, above all, has the task of showing that modern natural science must allow itself to be corrected by spiritual science for true knowledge to be attained. Oetinger strove for something different. He worked to prove that the spiritual world must be contacted if one is to attain an understanding of the Bible, or scriptures, especially the New Testament. Richard Rothe puts it beautifully:

> To understand this, one must assume the frame of mind [which was that of Oetinger] that admits, in its whole consciousness, that regarding the Holy Scriptures a full, complete, and therefore real understanding of them is still lacking, that the explanations given by the churches do not contain it.... [Rothe goes on to say:] Perhaps I can best make this clear by relating my own experience of more than thirty years of the Bible and, particularly, the New Testament, as well as the words of the Saviour and the Epistles of Paul. The more I study the Scriptures, with the help of the commentaries, the more I am impressed with the lively sense of their exuberant fullness, not just because of the inexhaustible ocean of feeling that surges through them, but equally by the thoughts contained in the words I encounter. I stand before them with a key put in my hand by the church, which has tested it for many centuries. I cannot exactly say that it does not fit; even less can I say that it is the right one. It has caused an opening, but only with the help of the power I use in the unlocking. Our traditional exegesis (I do not refer to recent doctrine) gives me some understanding of the Scriptures, but does not satisfy for a full and complete understanding. It is certainly able to draw out the general content of the thoughts, but cannot give any reason for the peculiar form in which the thoughts appear. It seems to me that there is a blossom flowering above and beyond the given exposition. This remains as an unexplained residue left behind the written word, and this puts the Bible Commentators and those to whom they refer in a very awkward position, however well they may have

accomplished their task in other respects. As a matter of fact, they have merely allowed the Lord and his Apostles to say exactly what the commentators wish them to say, and they have done this so clumsily—or perhaps we should say so wonderfully—that matters are made unnecessarily difficult to understand for those who read them.

The very large number of books comprising our exegetic literature deserves a serious reproach, since they speak with so little clarity and polish about such incomparably important matters and such an incomparably important object. Who does not feel that this blame is deserved? True Bible readers receive the unequivocal impression that the words are correct just as they are, and that this is not some meaningless scroll from which commentators must first cut away the wild branches before being able to penetrate the power of the thoughts contained within. They sense that the usual methods of these people—of sweeping away the dust from these documents because of their great age before they interpret them—simply tends to wipe away the imperishable springtime brilliance that has shone in eternal youth for thousands of years. Let the masters of Bible commentaries laugh as much as they wish; it remains a fact that there is something written between the lines of the Bible text that, with all their art, they are unable to decipher. Nevertheless, this is, above all, what we should be able to read if we wish to understand the altogether unique setting in which—only in the Holy Scriptures—the now-familiar thoughts of divinely manifested truth can be found, in characteristic contradistinction to anything else of the kind.

Our interpreters merely point to the figures standing in the foreground of the Scripture's images. They omit completely the background, with its wonderfully formed mountains in the far distance, and its brilliant dark-blue sky flecked with clouds. Yet, from this, that unique and magic light that illumines falls on each of us when we have understood what is truly an enigma to us. The peculiar basic thoughts and concepts in the Scriptures that underlie the unexpressed assumptions are lacking; and at the time there is a lack of soul, of the inner connection of the separate element of the biblical thoughts, which should bind them together organically. No wonder, then, that there are hundreds of passages in our Bible that remain without interpretation and are never properly understood, or not understood completely in all the minute details of their features. No wonder there are so many passages with a host of different given interpretations, ceaselessly disputed over for countless ages. No wonder at all; for they are certainly all wrong, because they are all inexact, only approximate, giving the meaning only as a whole, not in detail. We approach biblical text with the alphabet of our own concepts of God and the world, in all good faith, as though it was so obvious that it could not be otherwise. We take it for granted that Bible commentators—who, as silent observers, are at the back of all they think and write and illuminate—share the same opinion. However, this is an unfortunate illusion of which we should have been cured long ago by experiences.

Our key does not unlock; the right key had been lost, and until we find it again our investigations will find no green branch. We lack a fundamental concept of the Bible, not expressly given in the text itself, but as long as we make our research without the system that can be found therein, and that is not in our schools, the Bible must remain a half-closed book. We should study it with concepts fundamentally different from those we now cultivate as the only possibility. No matter what they are or where they are discovered, one thing is very certain from the whole concord of the melody of the Bible in its natural fullness: these concepts must be more realistic and more "substantial." This is my own individual opinion, and while far from wishing to force it on those to whom it is foreign, I must believe that Oetinger would understand and assure me that it was the same for him. Among all the many arguments that will be raised against me, I can still count one, if not many of my contemporaries, who will stand by me in this; I refer to the celebrated Dr. Beck of Tübingen.[6]

Oetinger had hoped he could reach an understanding of the Bible on trying to arouse concepts of a still-living nature in the twilight days in which he and Saint-Martin lived; he hoped to make them living to himself, so that he might enter a living connection with the spiritual world, being thus able to understand the true language of the Bible. His assumption in practice was this: with merely abstract intellectual ideas, it is impossible to understand the most important things in the Bible, especially in the New Testament. He believed that we can hope to understand the New Testament only if we realize that it arose from direct vision of the spiritual world itself and that no commentaries or exegeses are needed; but, above all, that we should learn to read the New Testament. With this object, he sought for a *Philosophia sacra*. He did not intend for this philosophy to be the pattern for those that came after, but one in which was inscribed what human beings can truly experience by living in contact with the spiritual world.

Today, those of us who love to shed the light of natural science with the research of spiritual science can no longer speak as Saint-Martin does; neither can we speak of the Gospels as Oetinger did, and even less like Bengel. The edition of the New Testament published by Bengel will still be of use; but people today have no use at all for the Apocalypse, of which he thought so much. In this, Bengel greatly stressed calculation; he figured out the periods of history in this way. He considered one number especially important. This alone is of course enough to make those of modern ideas view Bengel as crazy, eccentric, or foolish. According to his calculations, 1836 was to hold special importance in the development of humanity. He made profound calculations. He lived in the first half of the eighteenth century and

---

6   Probably Dr. Johann Tobias Beck, one of the most prominent Protestant
     theologians of the 19th century, who wrote numerous books.

was a hundred years removed from 1836. He figured this out in his own way by considering matters historically.

However, if we go more deeply into the question and are not as "clever" as the modern mind, we realize that our good Bengel was only six years off in his calculation. His error was caused by using the wrong year for the founding of Rome, which can easily be proved. The intended result of his calculation was 1842, the year we have given for the materialistic crisis. Bengel, the teacher of Oetinger, referred to that profound incision in time; but, in his search for weighty concepts he went too far and thought too heavily; thus, he figured that something very special would take place in the course of outer history, something like a final day. But it was only the last day of the ancient wisdom.

Thus, my dear friends, we see the decline of a theosophical age soon after our own time. Nonetheless, when historians or philosophers write about these persons at all today, they devote no more than a couple of lines to them, and these generally tell us very little. Yet, in their day these people had a very far-reaching, profound influence. If anyone today tries to reveal the meaning of the second part of *Faust* and finds it as given in the many commentaries, we cannot be surprised that:

> That mind alone never loses hope,
> That keeps to the shallows eternally,
> Grabs, with eager hand, the wealth it sees,
> And rejoices at the worms for which it gropes![7]

In this second part of *Faust*, there is an enormous amount of esoteric wisdom and rendering of occult facts, though expressed in truly German poetic form. All this would be inconceivable if it had not been preceded by the world of which I have given you only the two principal examples. People today have no idea of

---

7   "Dem Kopf nicht alle Hoffnung schwindet, der immerfort an schalem Zeuge klebt, mit gier-ger Hand nach Schätzen gräbt und froh ist, wenn er Regenwürmer findet." *Faust* (trans. A. S. Kline), part 1, scene 1, lines 602–605. http://www.scribd.com/doc/72912782/Goethe-s-Faust-Part-I-II.

how much was still known of the spiritual world even in relatively recent times, or that much of that belief was shed only in
recent decades. It is certainly very important to fix our attention
occasionally on these facts, because we—who now learn to read
the Gospels with the help of spiritual science—are just beginning
to learn again how to read the Scriptures.

There is a very remarkable sentence in Oetinger. In his writings, we find it quoted again and again, though never understood.
This sentence alone should suffice to make those who have insight
say that Oetinger is one of the greatest spirits of humanity. The
sentence says, "Matter is the end of the ways of God." It was possible only for a very highly developed soul to have provided such
a definition of matter, which corresponds so clearly to what spiritual science also knows—such a definition is possible only from
one who was in a position to understand how the Divine spiritual creative forces function and focus to bring about a material
structure such as the human being, who in form is the expression
of an enormous concentration of forces.

If you read what takes place at the beginning of the conver-
sation between Capesius and Benedictus in my second mystery
drama, and how the relationship between the macrocosm to
humankind is there developed, which causes Capesius to be ill,
you will be able to form a concept of how these things can be
translated into our words and expressed according to our present
spiritual science. This is what Oetinger expressed in his significant words, which can be understood only by rediscovering it:
"Matter is the end of God's path." Even here, it is true that, as
in the words of Saint-Martin, we can no longer speak this way
today. Anyone who uses such words must wish to preserve something that can no longer be understood today.

Not only have our concepts been greatly transformed, but our
feelings have been changed very greatly. Just consider a typical
person of modern times, one who is really a practical example of
this age, and imagine what this individual's impressions would
be when picking up Saint-Martin's *Errors and the Truth* and

encountering this sentence: "Human beings are preserved from knowing the principle of their outer corporeality; if they were to become acquainted with it, for the very shame they could never look at another uncovered person." In an age when a culture of nudity is encouraged even on a stage, as is done by the most modern people, of course we could make nothing of such a statement. Yet, just consider; a great philosopher who understands the world, Saint-Martin, tells us that a greater feeling of shame would make us blush to look upon the human form. Saint-Martin found this completely understandable.

You will have observed that today I initially wanted to draw your attention to something extremely significant that has now vanished. Moreover, I wanted you to notice the fact that a language was spoken then that is different from the way we speak now. We are required to speak differently. The possibility of thinking in a way that corresponds to that language has vanished. Both in Oetinger and in Saint-Martin, we find that matters were not thought through to their end; they could be thought through further and be discussed further, though not by a modern thinker. I might go even farther and say that we need not go into these things today when studying the conundrums of the world; rather we must understand ourselves through the concepts of our own day, not through old ones. Consequently, I always give much stress to the necessity of connecting all our spiritual-scientific work with modern ideas.

Regardless of how much we try now to fall back into those old ideas, it is remarkable that they are not played out. In themselves, they show that much more could be gained by thinking further along those lines. Because today we hold the strange belief that people have always thought just as we do today; we have no concept of how closely those concepts were connected with universal consciousness. The typical person, to whom I have already referred, thinks as follows: "I call the white powdered particles in the salt shaker, 'salt.'" Such a person is even aware that different languages use different names for salt, but one nonetheless assumes that this has always represented what we see it as today. This is not the case, however. Even the most uneducated peasants of the seventeenth and eighteenth centuries, and even more recently, had a much more comprehensive concept of "salt." They had the kind of concept to which Saint-Martin concentrated further; theirs was not our current materialistic idea, and when they spoke of "salt" they meant something related to spiritual life. Words then were not so material as they are today; they did not refer to a direct, separate substance.

I have discussed these matters today to show that we must now speak in a different way because we stand in the dawn, even as they then stood in the evening twilight. I also want to approach them now from yet another perspective. I would like to go back to the strange fact that, according to the modern view of things—from which the development of spiritual science must free itself—it would seem useless to go deeply into the nature of Bengel's, Oetinger's, Saint-Martin's, and others' ideas of their time. When we speak to educated people today, we must speak of the metabolic body, the rhythmic body, and the nervous system. We can no longer talk about the mercury body, the sulfur body, and the salt body. Such concepts, which were comprehensible in the age of Paracelsus, Jakob Böhme, Saint-Martin, and Oetinger, can no longer be understood today.

Nevertheless, it is not a waste of time to study these matters, not even if it were impossible to speak to cultured people today by these means. I am willing to acknowledge that it would not be wise to throw the old ideas of mercury, sulfur, and salt into modern thought; it would not be good or right to do so. Those who can feel the pulse of their time would not make the mistake of wanting to resurrect those old concepts, as is done in certain so-called esoteric societies that attach great weight to decorating themselves with old vignettes. Nonetheless, it is very important to regain the language that is no longer spoken, because Saint-Martin, Oetinger, and in more ancient times Paracelsus and Jakob Böhme by no means exhausted it.

Now, read in the Gospels how Christ says to the Disciples: "Ye are the salt of the Earth" (Matt. 5:13). Well, if these words are read with their present meaning, we do not get the words spoken by Christ, because the word *salt* was then understood quite naturally as referring to the whole configuration of the soul. Some people may be very broad-minded on the subject, but that is not enough. To evoke a similar feeling in people today, *salt* must be translated differently. This applies to many of the old records, but above all to the Scriptures. Many mistakes have been made in this very respect. Thus, it is easy to understand why Oetinger made so many historical studies, trying to get at whatever was concealed behind the value of words, and to get at the right feeling for them. Of course, in the present time a mind like his would be considered mad. He closed himself up in his laboratory, not just for weeks but for whole months, making alchemical experiments and studying cabalistic books, simply to discover how the words in a given sentence should be understood. All his efforts were directed toward the meaning of the words of holy writ.

Why is this? Yes, why? People today no longer speak that way. That language could fall into disuse and, at best, one could study the historical phenomenon of how it was possible for a historic period not to live out its full life. How did it come to pass that something still remains that might be carried further, but that has nonetheless come to a standstill? How does this happen? What is the underlying cause?

It may well be that if we could learn all there is to be learned, even without including these concepts, no one would be able to understand us. Here, however, something comes to light that has enormous significance. The living no longer speak of these concepts and do not need to use them. For the dead, however, for those who have passed through the portals of death, the language of these ideas is of all the more importance. If we have a chance to make ourselves understood by the dead or by certain other spirits of the spiritual world, we come to recognize that in a certain respect we need to learn that language, which has not been exhausted but has now died out of the earthly physical life of the material plane. It is among those who have passed through the portal of death that what lives and stirs in these concepts will become a living language, the current language they seek. The more we have tried to realize what was once thought, felt, and understood in these concepts, the more we can make ourselves understood by the spirits who have passed the portals of death. It is then easier to have a mutual understanding.

The peculiar and remarkable secret is therefore revealed—that a certain form of thought lives on this Earth up to only a certain point. It does not then develop further on Earth, but attains a further stage of perfection among those who pass into the intermediate life between death and rebirth. No one should believe that it is necessary only to learn what we can today about the formation of sulfur, quicksilver (mercury is not quicksilver), and salt; these concepts alone would not be enough to form a relationship with the dead through their language. However, if we can absorb these thoughts, as did Paracelsus, Jakob Böhme, and especially the almost superabundant fruitfulness of Saint-Martin, Oetinger, and Bengel, one perceives that a bridge is established between this world and that other. Regardless of how people may laugh at Bengel's calculations, which, of course, have no tangible value to outer physical life, those living between death and rebirth find them to have great significance and meaning. "Incisions" in time, the date of which Bengel tried to calculate and was only six years off, have very profound significance in that other world.

You can see that the world here on the physical plane and the world of the spirit are not so connected that we can form a bridge between them through abstract formulae; rather, they hang together in a concrete way. Something that, in a sense, loses its meaning here rises into the spiritual world and lives on there together with the dead, while with the living it must be succeeded by a different phase.

REFERENCES AND RELATED READING

Rudolf Steiner. *Death as Metamorphosis of Life: Including "What Does the Angel Do in our Astral Body?" & "How Do I Find Christ?"* Great Barrington, MA: SteinerBooks, 2008.

——. *The Education of the Child and Early Lectures on Education.* Hudson, NY: Anthroposophic Press, 1996.

——. *Four Mystery Dramas: The Portal of Initiation; The Soul's Probation; The Guardian of the Threshold; The Soul's Awakening.* Great Barrington, MA: SteinerBooks, 2007.

——. *How to Know Higher Worlds: A Modern Path of Initiation.* Great Barrington, MA: Anthroposophic Press, 1994.

——. *The Influence of the Dead on Destiny.* Great Barrington, MA: SteinerBooks, 2007.

——. *Intuitive Thinking as a Spiritual Path: A Philosophy of Freedom.* Great Barrington, MA: Anthroposophic Press, 1995.

——. *An Outline of Esoteric Science.* Great Barrington, MA: Anthroposophic Press, 1997.

——. *The Riddle of Man: From the Thinking, Observation, and Contemplations of a Series of German and Austrian Personalities.* Spring Valley, NY: Mercury Press, 1990.

——. *Spiritualism, Madame Blavatsky and Theosophy: An Eyewitness View of Occult History.* Great Barrington, MA: SteinerBooks, 2002.

——. *The Stages of Higher Knowledge: Imagination, Inspiration, Intuition.* Great Barrington, MA: SteinerBooks, 2009.

——. *Staying Connected: How to Continue Your Relationships with Those Who Have Died.* Great Barrington, MA: Anthroposophic Press, 1999.

——. *Theosophy: An Introduction to the Spiritual Processes in Human Life and in the Cosmos.* Great Barrington, MA: Anthroposophic Press, 1994.

CPSIA information can be obtained at www.ICGtesting.com
Printed in the USA
BVOW070318230212

283620BV00002B/5/P